P9-CSH-093

9/16/11

Susan,

Wishing you

continued success as

you unleash the power

of IT across your

organization!

Unleashing the Power of IT

Unleashing the Power of IT

Bringing People, Business, and Technology Together

DAN ROBERTS

WILEY

John Wiley & Sons, Inc.

Copyright © 2011 by Ouellette & Associates Consulting, Inc. All rights reserved.

Published by John Wiley & Sons, Inc., Hoboken, New Jersey.

Published simultaneously in Canada.

No part of this publication may be reproduced, stored in a retrieval system, or transmitted in any form or by any means, electronic, mechanical, photocopying, recording, scanning, or otherwise, except as permitted under Section 107 or 108 of the 1976 United States Copyright Act, without either the prior written permission of the Publisher, or authorization through payment of the appropriate per-copy fee to the Copyright Clearance Center, Inc., 222 Rosewood Drive, Danvers, MA 01923, (978) 750-8400, fax (978) 646-8600, or on the Web at www.copyright.com. Requests to the Publisher for permission should be addressed to the Permissions Department, John Wiley & Sons, Inc., 111 River Street, Hoboken, NJ 07030, (201) 748-6011, fax (201) 748-6008, or online at http://www.wiley.com/go/permissions.

Limit of Liability/Disclaimer of Warranty: While the publisher and author have used their best efforts in preparing this book, they make no representations or warranties with respect to the accuracy or completeness of the contents of this book and specifically disclaim any implied warranties of merchantability or fitness for a particular purpose. No warranty may be created or extended by sales representatives or written sales materials. The advice and strategies contained herein may not be suitable for your situation. You should consult with a professional where appropriate. Neither the publisher nor author shall be liable for any loss of profit or any other commercial damages, including but not limited to special, incidental, consequential, or other damages.

For general information on our other products and services or for technical support, please contact our Customer Care Department within the United States at (800) 762-2974, outside the United States at (317) 572-3993 or fax (317) 572-4002.

Wiley also publishes its books in a variety of electronic formats. Some content that appears in print may not be available in electronic books. For more information about Wiley products, visit our web site at www.wiley.com.

Library of Congress Cataloging-in-Publication Data

Roberts, Dan (Dan D.),
  Unleashing the Power of IT: Bringing People, Business, and Technology Together / Dan Roberts.
      p. cm
      Includes bibliographical references and index.
  ISBN 978-0-470-92042-8 (hardback); 978-1-118-04447-6 (ebk); 978-1-118-04448-3 (ebk); 978-1-118-04450-6 (ebk)
  1. Information technology—Management.   I. Title.
  HD30.2.R6277 2011
  004.068--dc22

                                                              2010050381

Printed in the United States of America

10 9 8 7 6 5 4 3 2 1

Contents

Foreword

A funny thing has happened to business over the last 30 years. In many cases, technology has become the face of the company, both for internal clients and all the way out to the end customer. Tracking shipments through Fedex.com? Ordering books at Amazon.com? That interface *is* the business. Meanwhile, in the same time frame, a funny thing has happened to technology—the success of implementations hinges more on human behavior and well-executed processes than the performance of development languages and database design.

I can fairly say I was there when the business world began to discover data, a key factor in today's high valuation of technology. When I first started in IT, mainframes hummed away in a darkened room, and we worked behind a curtain of mystique, automating traditional business processes for technologically unsophisticated users. But as time moved on, projects grew more complex and strategic. During my days as a senior executive and CIO, I helped introduce FedEx's worldwide package-tracking system, oversaw the implementation of AT&T and Sprint's customer billing and marketing systems and drove the technology strategy as Wellpoint grew from an $18 billion to $76 billion health insurance giant.

Fast-forward a few years, and we reach the age of the Internet, rampant mobilization and new computing architectures like cloud computing—not to mention steady progress in database design and programming languages—to the point where today, technology has never been more complex and yet more integral to most people's lives. Meanwhile, when it comes to technology savvy, all the players—internal clients, business leaders and external customers—are smarter than they've ever been.

What all this means for IT leaders is that the demands have never been greater. And yet I see a disturbing trend in the increasing scarcity of what I call "the complete CIO." This is someone who can sit at the table with the C suite, with a complete command of the IT strategy, masterful knowledge of the business strategy and the ability to synchronize and coordinate the two. This same person should thoroughly understand the business the company is in and view it through the client's and the customer's eyes. He or she needs to comprehend the entire technology spectrum and have the mindset and skills to see projects through to completion. Unfortunately, this is the kind of rising IT leader that seems to be in diminishing supply, these days.

In the large and complex projects in which I've been involved, technology has generally never been the salient point of failure. It's always some aspect of the human equation that falters – not having an enterprise view, not being politically astute, not knowing how or when to push back on client requests in a positive way. And today, I see up-and-coming IT leaders continually repeating the same mistakes. I'm not sure if this is true for other professions, but what we lack in IT is a vehicle for transferring knowledge from a collective memory bank of lessons learned, to grow and evolve into something better, with each passing year.

Until now. In its new book, Ouellette & Associates has successfully captured years of experience in one easily digested but highly detailed, very true-to-reality book. Finally, someone has recorded what it takes to move beyond the behaviors that lead to project delays and cost overruns, and transform IT into the mature, evolved profession that those who are committed to it—and those who rely on it—truly deserve. O&A has compiled, in one place, decades of lessons learned, recipes and prescriptions for doing IT right, indeed, to become "the complete CIO."

Reading this book was a fascinating experience for me—it felt both like a collection of memories from my time in the industry and a searing look at the present, as well. The human side of the IT enterprise is where the work needs to be done, and that's exactly where the authors focus for creating a transformed IT workforce and culture.

IT transformation doesn't happen overnight, and the book's layout takes that into consideration. Read straight through, the book moves from the stage-setting topics of team transformation and a service-oriented, consultative mindset, to the more advanced skill of negotiation. With that foundation, it tunnels into project management and requirements-gathering and then pops back out to the more sophisticated area of politically savvy. It is only once you have these skills mastered that you can move on to the last three areas explored, which are marketing your newly developed value, managing service providers and—finally—driving change management efforts. For each skill, you can dip your toe in the water, get comfortable and then move to the next stage.

At the same time, I've always believed in tackling large and complex jobs by breaking them into smaller, logical pieces, and the authors have also accomplished that. You can go right to Chapter 4 to learn about consultant skills or burrow into Chapter 9 to learn how to market IT. Checklists, recipes and diagrams enable you to put new insights immediately into action. And all the while, you get the distinct feeling that these people get it—they've seen it before. They've been there.

I see the need for this book in almost every company I work with today—and in retrospect, the ones I worked with in the past. It is my firm belief that many senior IT professionals have the capacity to be the "complete CIOs" that business needs today, if they would give themselves, and their staff, the chance.

It's easy to say, "I don't have the time" for the transformation espoused in this book. But if everyone could do even half of what this book advocates, we could begin to pass the baton of experience onto the next generation of IT leaders, who could go on to enjoy the fulfilling career in IT that people like me have had the honor to experience.

I think anyone who—like me—has spent the last three decades in IT would concur: With this book, O&A has done a great service for IT professionals. I'd urge anyone who is serious about IT to start the transformation the book describes to unleash the power of their own career.

Ron J. Ponder
The Ponder Group

Preface

Positioning IT as Provider of Choice: Moving Beyond IT and Business Alignment

We at Ouellette & Associates Consulting, Inc. (O&A) are committed more than ever to preparing IT leaders and their staffs and organizations for the next phase of IT's evolution and a successful future. This is particularly true as forward-thinking IT leaders change their focus from "aligning IT with the business," to instilling a philosophy that says, "We are the business." With the growing belief that IT and business alignment has exacerbated the us-versus-them issue, IT leaders today are becoming laser-focused on ensuring that IT is integrated into the business.

Since 1984, our tagline has been, "Developing the Human Side of Technology," and never has this mantra been more important to IT than it is today. We've been fortunate to work with more than 3,000 IT organizations representing all industries, led by progressive IT leaders who are dedicated to changing the culture of their IT organizations, whether their staffs numbered 10 or 10,000. This book is based on these industry pioneers and their passion for and commitment to moving their organizations from reactive, technology-centric order takers to consultative and service-minded—in short, organizations that position internal IT as the business's technology provider of choice.

While other managers immediately cut their professional or organizational development budget at the first sign of economic distress, these savvy leaders invested in their people during both good and bad economic times. Through their leadership and professional development initiatives, they spearheaded and sponsored their own personal transformations and then proceeded to help their departments reach their full potential.

A Unique Approach: Putting the Book into Action

Others have written about the changing field of IT, but O&A's approach is unique. For one, it's written by a team of highly experienced subject matter experts who have lived in the trenches, worked with world-class IT organizations and—for the first time—have committed their insights and experience to paper. Together, these seasoned professionals represent more than 200 years of experience in the real-world IT trenches and as consultants and trainers, helping tens of thousands of IT professionals change how they do business, both individually and organizationally. Because they've walked the walk as IT practitioners, leaders, and consultants, they write with a voice of authority that comes from experience.

On a personal level, I have contributed to several books that have been very well received by our industry. I am extremely excited about *Unleashing the Power of IT: Bringing People, Business, and Technology Together,* based on the reviews and feedback provided by several respected industry leaders, and am confident about the value it's going to bring to the IT industry and profession.

Our approach is also unique because the advice and guidance we provide are not just words that lie on the page. You won't hear us promoting the latest management fad, promising silver-bullet solutions to the challenges you face as an IT leader. We strived to write a book that was practical and immediately applicable. How many times have you read a business book, agreed with most everything it said and then discovered you didn't have much, if anything, tangible to apply? This book, like the proven workshops and services it is based on, is designed for you to begin using what you've learned immediately. Rather than writing from a 30,000-foot level, we have combined big-picture context with specific advice you can use in your next planning session, staff meeting, or client interaction.

At the end of each chapter, you'll find a "Top Ten" list summarizing the chapter and providing you with immediate, actionable takeaways. We will also prompt you to note a few specific actions you plan to take based on what you just read.

We also include a "Putting the Book into Action" chapter, in which we illustrate how three of our clients have successfully used our workshops, certification programs, consulting services, and books to turn their IT organizations into strategic business partners.

This format aligns with our overall philosophy of helping our clients "learn how to fish." At O&A, we've never been big fans of the traditional consulting model that makes clients be dependent. This may be good for revenue generation, but it's an approach that's never sat well with us. Our focus has always been on helping our clients become self-sufficient. This book will seek to do the same.

This book is also not going to tell you everything there is to know about IT culture change. It would take several books and more time than you have to cover everything there is to know about this topic. Our goal instead is to help you be effective, to jumpstart your journey, and to build and sustain your momentum. If you've already begun, then this book will add to your toolkit. If you're one of those rare IT leaders who've successfully transformed your IT organization, you already recognize that success is a journey and not a destination. I hope you'll meld our experiences and best practices with your own to take your organization to the next level.

We base the book on proven approaches that generate results. O&A's clients have applied and sustained the teachings in
this book, and by doing so, they've positioned their organizations for the future. They've chosen to focus on developing the
"human side" of IT rather than "fixing" IT by applying the latest
technology, methodology, framework, or management guru
fad. They've discovered that success is based not on a big-bang
theory but by executing many little things every day. These
small wins add up and build momentum from the top down and
from the bottom up.

That's why we believe that by reading this book and acting
on its advice, you too can build strong relationships with your
business partners and earn a seat at the table of strategic decision making. You too will be perceived as an effective commu-
nicator, tactful negotiator, and influential opinion leader across
your organization. And your IT organization will also be positioned as the IT provider of first choice.

Acknowledgments

A book project is a major undertaking that requires the efforts of many great people to bring it to fruition. Looking back, we actually started work on this book in 1984 when we began partnering with our clients in support of their transformation efforts.

We want to thank our world-class clients who include us in their transformation initiatives. We consider ourselves extremely fortunate to work with some of the most savvy IT leaders in our industry; some have sponsored our work at two, three and even four companies. Without them our work would not be possible and this book could never have been written.

Three CIOs have provided us with an inside look at how they have transformed their IT organizations, applying the concepts of this book to build a high performing culture. In Chapter 12, you will read about the real-world success stories of Marriott Corporation CIO Carl Wilson, St. Luke's Health System CIO Adrienne Edens and Bowdoin College CIO Mitch Davis. You will no doubt enjoy reading about the transformational journeys of these visionary CIOs and benefit from their years of experience, keen insights and the best practices they leveraged along the way.

Several other clients were kind enough to review and critique our manuscript, provide encouragement and offer detailed feedback that greatly enhanced the book you now have in your hands. These highly regarded IT leaders include: Roger Agee—JELD WEN, Inc.; Ben Berry—Oregon Department of Transportation;

Scott Culbertson—UGI Utilities; Inc.; Rick Giese—Great Lakes Educational Loan Services; Cam Henderson—Portland General Electric; Don Desiderato—Novarica; Alan Guibord—The Advisory Council; Don Imholz—Centene Corporation; Laurie Koetting—Computer World Services Corp; Barbara Koster—Prudential; Chris Loizides—The MITRE Corporation; Deane Morrison—Capital Region Health Care; Eric Nilson—Jet Propulsion Laboratory; Ron Ponder, The Ponder Group; Guy Russo—CommunityAmerica Credit Union; Wade Vann—Augusta Sportswear; Sharon Waid—Boston Financial; Lorena Weaver—Allianz Life; and Meg Williams—Columbus Regional Airport Authority.

We also want to thank our families who support the work we do with clients. Without their support on the home front while we are traveling and logging crazy hours, we could not do the work that we love so much.

Tackling a book project with multiple authors is a blessing and a curse. It's a blessing because you can leverage the knowledge and experiences of many subject matter experts. It's a curse when you try to weave different personalities and voices together to ensure consistency for the reader. Given this challenge, we want to thank Mary Brandel because without her writing talents, this book would not have become a reality. Her ability to capture our real-world experiences and personalities is a gift. Her ability to find a common voice for our readers was incredibly important.

And many thanks are extended to the great folks at Wiley. We could not ask for a publishing partner that is more talented, dedicated and professional. We are proud to be part of Wiley's CIO Book Series.

CHAPTER 1

Creating Your Twenty-First Century Workforce and Culture

There has never been a better time to be an information technology (IT) professional. That's right! While prognosticators have loudly predicted the demise of IT, I firmly believe there has never been a more exciting or auspicious time to be in this profession.

That may sound strange to some of you IT veterans out there. You may remember the good ol' days of electronic data processing when IT professionals were safe behind the glass walls, free to focus on technology, without interference from those pesky end users. Or perhaps you remember being the hero in the late 1990s, riding in on a white horse to save the world from the Y2K coding debacle. Then there were the wild, early days of the Internet, when being a techie was suddenly cool.

For those who long for any of those days, I can appreciate your disdain for my optimism. You've weathered the worst recession we've seen in our lifetime, the outsourcing that leveled many of your staffs, the questioning of IT's value and the return-on-investment scrutiny that continues today. You're now witnessing the encroachment of consumer technology into the enterprise, rampant proliferation of as-a-service computing models, virtualization of nearly everything, and the growing assumption that applications and data can and should be accessed and run from anywhere, on anything.

But still, I don't think I'm being naïve. Though the last few years have been riddled with doubt, disappointment, and discomfort, they also produced an awareness in most of the business world that technology can be a game-changer. From a business leader's perspective, market forces such as globalization, consumerization, and increasingly savvy consumers have turned technology into a key differentiator as companies seek to expand into new markets and create a competitive advantage. Cutthroat competition is forcing continuous innovation, and government regulations are driving constant introspection—all fueled by technology. Corporate strategies are increasingly influenced by the desire to interact with customers through online communities and use the social Web to enhance customer loyalty and find new product and service innovations. Meanwhile, particularly as Gen Y and even younger employees fill the payrolls, people have no patience with "the IT computer guys" who say, "We can't do that."

At one and the same time, the people in charge of technology are expected to be technologically advanced, business-minded, customer-focused, and financially astute. Technology leaders are expected to reduce costs, increase productivity, drive innovation, and help the business identify and pursue new business opportunities and customers. In the face of unforgiving competition, rampant globalization, and demanding customers, business leaders now know that it's absolutely essential to have a strong, active partner keeping a firm hand on the decisions and strategies surrounding information technology.

Of course, there have never been more options to consider when it comes to doing just that. IT faces competition from internal shadow groups, vendors and consultants, service providers, cloud providers, and offshorers, all promising to do it faster, cheaper, better. But still, I firmly believe that IT organizations can be well positioned to compete as their companies' value-added provider of choice—*if and only if* they're ready to take a hard look at themselves and make some changes, both in regard to how they approach their work and the personal skill set they consider essential to tackling the demands of an ever-changing business environment. The bottom line is, the IT professional of the past won't cut it in today's corporate world.

Core Skills for Success

To remain viable, IT leaders need to proactively transform their organizations and cultures. To accomplish this, they need to develop an IT workforce that has the new mindset, skill set, and tool set necessary for success, such as communicating, relationship-building, collaborating, managing change, marketing, negotiating, and the like. These are the skills that are necessary for effectively filling the growing percentage of IT jobs that are business-facing.

You've heard this before, but today, it's no longer just a suggestion; what have historically been termed *soft skills* are the very ones that will drive IT to the level it needs to reach for it to be viable in the future. In fact, savvy IT leaders no longer use the term *soft skills* when referring to these key capabilities. They call them *core skills* because they're the very ones needed to achieve hard results.

If you step back for a minute, the need to evolve shouldn't be surprising. The IT profession is really still in its infancy. It's only a few decades old—a new kid on the block compared to its peers in other business areas that have had centuries to develop. I can imagine a time in the future when we'll look back at the second half of the twentieth century as the time when IT was just cutting its teeth.

In some ways, IT professionals are now living through the tough teenage years of their profession. They're wrestling with internal turmoil they often don't understand while defiantly ignoring the advice and experience provided by their external environment. Like teenagers, they want so badly to be independent and earn the respect of their peers and elders. However, their erratic, mercurial behavior and unpredictability continue to demonstrate their immaturity.

The exciting news for IT professionals is that they're poised to enter adulthood. And this new era will have less to do with a command-and-control or bits-and-bytes mindset and more to do with being collaborative and versatile business partners.

A Consistent Terminology

Part of the value we bring to our clients when helping them with their IT culture change efforts is the introduction of a consistent vocabulary. In this book, we will frequently use words and phrases that might mean different things to different people. Therefore, I want to define a few of these here for you:

- *IT.* We will commonly refer to *IT* as the organization responsible for managing and delivering technology and related services.
- *Client versus Customer.* We will refer to *clients* or *business partners* as those who are the beneficiaries of IT's products and services. When we use the term *customer,* it will refer to the "Big C" customers to whom our corporations provide products and services.
- *WIIFM ("wiff-em").* WIIFM stands for "What's in It for Me," an expression we want every IT professional to think about when considering a client's point of view. In other words, find out what matters to the client before expecting her to be motivated to act.

4

- *The Four Cs.* Each chapter is focused on helping you increase your staff's Competence, Confidence, Commitment, and Consistency in each area addressed.

We also reinforce some key concepts throughout the book. For example, you'll read a lot about the importance of teamwork and collaboration—not just with clients, but also with peers in IT. It's time for IT professionals to rid themselves of "us-versus-them" tendencies because to meet the needs of the business, everyone needs to row in the same direction.

Interpersonal skills also come up a lot. In fact, one of our consultants refers to his project management workshops as a "three-day charm school!" Interpersonal skills, or core skills as previously described, lead to strong relationships, which lead to trust, and with trust, we can overcome even our most difficult situations.

IT professionals tend not to like the touchy-feely stuff, but you'll also read a lot about empathy, an area of weakness in the IT profession. You'll find that empathy is less touchy-feely than you think and is actually a key tool for working through conflict, building relationships, and achieving your full potential. It's a matter of listening to the other person's perspectives and letting that person know you've heard and understand them. You don't even need to agree!

Who Will Benefit Most

A wide range of people will benefit from reading this book, including IT leaders holding titles from chief information officer (CIO), to business unit or regional information officer, to vice president, to director or manager of IT. Whether you are the CIO of a 10,000-person IT staff that spans the globe or a manager overseeing a local IT team, I am confident that you will

5

benefit from reading this book. We are excited to share the experience, best practices, and proven techniques that other IT leaders are using to reorient, reskill, and retool their IT workforce and build a new culture.

It's not only leaders who will benefit from this book. Whether you work in applications or the technology infrastructure side of the IT business—and whether you aspire to management or wish to be the most effective individual contributor you can be—this book will introduce anyone on the IT staff to the philosophies and skill sets that will help you meet the challenges of your profession. If you follow the latest research and read industry trade publications, you know that an increasing percentage of IT jobs and roles in the future are going to be client- and business-facing, and we will help you prepare for these new opportunities.

Leveraging This Book

We believe that each of the chapters in this book is important for success. That being said, we appreciate that every IT organization is in a different stage of their transformation evolution and that some chapters will be more immediately applicable than others. We also appreciate that it isn't feasible to effectively tackle all of these areas at once.

Therefore, we recommend that once you've read the book, you identify the two or three chapters that address the areas most pressing in your organization today. Make these a priority in your organization and strategy planning. Demonstrate your commitment and sponsorship by taking every opportunity to "walk the talk" and communicating these priorities to your people.

We also advise that you engage each level of your management team in your IT initiative, because they play a critical role in building a new culture. Include them in establishing priorities and determining action plans, and hold them accountable for achieving these priorities. Don't allow them to revert back to their technical comfort zones. Be sure to position your people for success by investing in them and providing them with the new skills and tools they'll need to be successful. This approach will help you address today's priorities while building momentum toward the future.

Warning! Do not start down this path unless you are seriously committed to sustaining it. If your efforts are not continued, you will add to the cynicism level created by past transformation initiatives that ended prematurely or were pushed aside by yet another flavor of the month. Slow and steady can win the race, but starting and stopping is not an option, as it will negatively affect your reputation and the credibility of IT across the enterprise.

So, let me modify the statement I made at the very beginning of this chapter. I still say there's never been a better time to be in IT, but I'll add that there's also never been a more challenging time in IT's short history. The question is, are you up for that challenge? Because if you are, we wish you success and are excited that you have included us in your transformation journey!

CHAPTER 2

Transforming Your IT Team

It's relatively easy—when you're on the outside looking in—to see when an industry or profession is in the midst of a revolutionary transformation. Journalists, for example, are currently facing identity crises as people flock to blogs for news and insights. The entertainment industry continues to evolve, as younger audiences spend more time with reality TV programs and amateur videos on the Web than with situation comedies on TV.

It's more difficult to have this perspective when it's your own profession that's undergoing radical change. But that's exactly what's happening in IT. In my nearly 30 years in corporate America—including 18 years in internal IT (five as a CIO) and four as an external consultant—I've seen the demands placed on IT leaders change from keeping the mainframes humming to leading high-performance organizations that partner with the business to consistently deliver successful solutions.

Many IT professionals are still evolving toward that role. But the fact is, IT leaders have no choice but to transform themselves and the organizations they lead. Today, business leaders require CIOs and other IT leaders not only to exercise exceptional leadership behaviors, but also to lead their teams in sustaining strong client partnerships, demonstrating business and financial acuity, executing successful projects, and delivering exceptional results.

And this transformation is hard work—it's threatening, humbling, and draining. It involves research, retooling, and missteps all along the way. This is especially true for the people I've seen promoted to the highest IT ranks based more on their technical prowess than their leadership capabilities. And often, these are the people who don't fully understand the need not only to undergo such a transformation themselves, but also to lead their IT groups to become high-performance organizations, as well. No wonder the average tenure of a CIO or CTO these days is just two to three years!

But as painful as this transformation might be, it's a necessary change for IT professionals who want a successful future in technology for themselves and the departments they lead.

I first got my feet wet in leading team transformations about 15 years ago, when I was working at a Fortune 500 company and found myself continually being put into positions to help turn departments around. My approach was a commonsense one; in each case, I'd look for what was broken and develop a plan to fix it.

As I saw each area reach its full potential and the positive impact that had on people's lives, I became even more motivated to fine-tune my skills to affect a faster turnaround the next time. It's so great to see people actually enjoy what they're doing! The positive energy is magnetic. Those experiences were a turning point for me, and I now consider that time as my "boot camp days" of learning about effective team transformation.

During that time, I developed what I call my recipe for transforming departments and teams. The best thing about it is that anyone with the right mindset can follow it. The recipe involves assessing your team's strengths and weaknesses through external feedback, developing a plan to overcome weaknesses, choosing a handful of top priorities, promoting the success stories and then refreshing that plan every six months after you determine what's working and what's not. Even if you're not in a blatant turnaround situation, it's my firm belief that no matter how well your team is operating, there's always room to raise the bar.

"Who, me?" I've heard many an IT leader say. "I don't have time to change, and I don't see the need to." And that may be true. But just to be sure, it's important to take a look inward. When I talk with IT leaders, I urge them to heed the following warning signs that signal a change is necessary:

- Client and executive dissatisfaction with IT performance and outcomes
- Strained client relationships
- Too many Number 1 priorities
- Missed IT goals, objectives, and metrics
- Inability to effectively position and sell IT ideas and solutions
- Missed project deadlines, budgets, and client-expected outcomes
- Talent shortfalls—absence of IT consultative, financial, project leadership, and business-savvy competencies and skills
- IT silos inhibiting teamwork, synchronization of efforts, and bidirectional communication
- IT resource constraint issues
- Unclear IT roles and responsibilities
- Inability to achieve agility, flexibility, and scalability
- Excessive system downtimes
- Difficulty in negotiating airtight vendor contracts and effectively managing vendor performance and results
- The perception of IT as commodity resources rather than competitive advantage enablers that deliver undisputed value

If any of these conditions sound familiar to you, then I urge you to start developing the mindsets and strategies that are necessary to be a high-performance leader. These mindsets have less to do with programming and system architectures and more to do with interpersonal skills, business knowledge, communication, critical thinking, and decision making.

And it's not just about transforming yourself—you need to build a culture of leadership throughout the IT organization. I've never met a successful IT leader who didn't also have a great leadership team. In fact, when I was interviewing for the CIO position I held for five years, I wrote down a list of ideas of what I would do if I were hired. Eight months into the job, I came across that piece of paper and had to laugh—all those ideas had been accomplished! But it wasn't all by me—it was due to the leadership team I'd put in place and the environment I'd created in which people could reach their full potential.

It's a basic tenet of IT leadership: You simply can't be effective if you don't foster a great team. Whether you've got a team of 500, 1,000, or just two, you can only perform as well as the weakest link. Unfortunately, I don't see a lot of collaborative teamwork happening in most IT organizations. Instead, I see territorial, silo-oriented attitudes toward resources, responsibilities, and budgets. I see people focused on their functional areas and rarely if ever taking the enterprise view. IT organizations have to wake up to the notion that none of us owns anything—it all belongs to the enterprise.

The entire IT organization needs to behave like a surgical team, in which everyone knows what needs to happen next and collaborates with precision. And just as a nurse seamlessly hands off equipment to the surgeon, IT professionals need to just as effectively complete their own hand-offs. In IT's case, that means reflexively asking questions like, "Who else will this affect?"; "Who else should be involved?"; "What resources do I need?"; and "Who do I need to talk to?" Once those questions are answered, it means following through with effective communication and ensuring the hand-off occurs. When this kind of collaboration occurs, no ball ever gets dropped!

Collaboration has to be encouraged at the highest levels of the enterprise, and rewards for teamwork have to be built into performance assessments. IT professionals need to know they're being measured based on their contribution to the greater good, not their own (or their team's) individual performance.

The cold, harsh truth is that technology executives who continue to ignore the need to transform themselves and their teams eventually become organizational casualties. But if you choose to embark on the road to high-performance leadership—and work with your people to impart the same competencies—your organization will be a force to be reckoned with.

How to Make This Transition: Learn to Think Differently

It's so easy to fall into old, comfortable habits. But as I work with IT leadership teams across the country, I find there are six mindset and behavioral changes that must precede a successful leadership transformation.

Mindset Change 1: Force Yourself to Plan and Think of the Big Picture

Like it or not, IT can no longer afford to be all things to all people. Given all the demands for technology-enabled business initiatives, it's actually beneficial to everyone—including your clients—to develop a strategy that's based on a set of clear, finite priorities formed by what's most important to the client, both within IT and out in the business. That way, if clients ask for systems or projects that are off the list, you can help them see for themselves where these requests fit in (or don't fit in) to the overall business strategy. When someone tries to add something to IT's plate, you can manage that situation effectively rather than running around fighting fires.

I often hear IT leaders say, "I could be more strategic if I just had more people to get things done." But it's a vicious cycle—without a strategy, you'll never have enough people, because it's impossible to "get it all done." The only way to line up your resources effectively is to identify priorities based on business strategy. In some cases, I've seen organizations discover they have extra resources, which enables them to volunteer for additional projects—doing wonders for their reputations.

The important thing is to have a collective, consolidated view of what IT needs to get done. And that view needs to extend across the entire organization—I've seen leaders make the mistake of letting each IT area identify its own list of priorities that eventually conflict with one another. Instead, the entire IT organization needs to develop one set of priorities, all focused on what's most important to the business.

Developing this list of priorities depends, of course, on getting out there and talking with clients on a frequent basis. IT leaders need to venture out into the business community and interact with peers and department heads on a formal and informal basis, and they need to encourage their staffs to mingle with their business clients, as well. This is so important that we've covered the topic of networking and building rapport in great depth in Chapter 4, which focuses on consulting skills.

In some cases, when you meet with business leaders, you may discover that they don't yet have a clear strategic plan themselves. But you absolutely can't take that as an excuse to not move forward. In fact, if you've established a strong level of trust as an IT leader, you're in a great position to encourage business leaders to develop a strategy and even facilitate the process of building one. They would come around quickly if you can articulate to them that without a strategy, there's no way to establish priorities, and without priorities, there's no way to assign resources to achieve the outcome they expect. People generally respond when they see the win in it for themselves.

Of course, this conversation can't even take place if you don't have a prior relationship with business leaders. So for some of us, the first step is identifying the people you need to develop a relationship with, whether in IT or in your client base, and then reaching out to them before you need something from them. It has to be genuine.

Mindset Change 2: Adopt a Proactive Approach

You simply can't be a leader if you assume a passive, victim's mentality. I see too many IT organizations that would rather point fingers, cast blame, and take the easy way out. But true leaders create the future, and that means doing the hard work of assessing the world around you and taking preemptive action. It may seem at first to be a much harder path to take, but it's ultimately much more satisfying to realize we can take actions that will affect the outcomes in our lives.

I've seen dysfunctional leaders who wait until they hear a critical mass of client complaints before they take steps to improve their department's level of service. Or they assume everything's going well because—rather than interacting with staff, clients, and fellow executives who could provide them with critical input—they're more comfortable sitting in their offices answering e-mail.

High-performance leaders, on the other hand, are always looking to raise the bar, before clients complain. They're socially aware, able to read the political landscape, and engage in social networks. Indeed, effective leaders spend much of their time working with people, including clients, other leaders, and their staff. They also make it part of their staff's performance reviews to report on what they've done to nurture their key relationships.

15

Mindset Change 3: Resist the Temptation to Delve into Tactics

Many IT leaders are techies at heart. They love jumping in and fighting fires when crises arise; in fact, they may even believe that no one else on their staff could resolve the problem as well as they can. Plus, it's fun being the hero, and it's definitely thrilling to rise to a demanding, immediate challenge.

However, it's not your job as an IT leader to react to short-term situations; you need to be strategizing about the future. If you don't do it, who else will?

In my leadership workshops, I consistently hear participants say they don't have time to engage in leadership activities. One told me he didn't have time for the "soft and fuzzy stuff" involved with building relationships. I tell these people there's something very wrong going on if that's the case. Perhaps they don't have an effective team in place, or perhaps they haven't created an environment in which the team knows what's expected of them and are accountable for their performance.

Others use "no time" as an excuse for their feeling that they hate pulling themselves out of technology work. They don't like solving problems that involve people; they'd rather work with technology, which is more cut and dried. If that's the case, a leadership position may just not be for them.

Very often, leaders would have the time if they managed their time better. It's amazing how terrible our time management skills can be, even at the highest positions in the company. For example, e-mail can be a real time-suck—it's all too easy to be drawn in by every new e-mail that crosses your screen. I recommend that leaders check it three times per day—once in the morning, once at noon, and once at night—and otherwise shut it off. Meetings are another one. I recommend creating agendas for our meetings and sticking to them. If you develop agendas in advance, people can be prepared, and meetings will progress more quickly and smoothly.

Becoming less tactical and more strategic also requires quiet time, so schedule some time for just thinking on your calendar. It's easy to let your calendar get filled by meetings—including meaningless ones, like vendor lunches—but you need to have the discipline to schedule time for strategic thinking, which might mean leaving the office and going somewhere offsite where you can find peace and quiet.

I know a CIO at a global company who visits client sites around the world to talk with them about their needs. When he returns, he schedules time on his calendar to review his notes and follow up with suggestions and strategies to fulfill those needs.

Delegation is another crucial tool for clearing time on your schedule. This, of course, requires having staffers whom you trust to lead in your place. As CIO, I used to have customers call me and ask that I, personally, get involved with something they wanted done. Even in those cases, I would sometimes delegate the work to a trusted staff member. I'd assure the client that they were in good hands and that I'd hand-chosen the best person for their needs. It's all how you frame it.

If you feel you're the only one who can jump in when problems arise, that's a warning sign. We may love being the hero and revel in resolving crises, but those are reactive activities, and we're consigned to be proactive leaders.

It's easy to think we don't have the time to do this leadership work, but the fact is, that's why we were hired; it's the value we bring. We need to take a close look at what we do with our time and clear the decks of non-value-add tasks by delegating to our staffs, managing our time more effectively, and analyzing whether certain tasks are even necessary.

Mindset Change 4: Be Candid with Yourself and Others

The best leaders I've seen have the courage to be candid, particularly when it comes to conflict. Generally, people don't like conflict and seek to avoid it, mainly because they don't know how to deal with it. Navigated well, however, conflict can actually be part of a very constructive process that ultimately leads to innovation. That means keeping emotions out of it and not taking disagreement personally. If there's something you don't think is working, say so. It's a coward's choice to verbally agree and then walk away full of resentment that you didn't get your way. Dealing with conflict is such an important skill that we've covered the topic of conflict management in Chapter 5, in which we focus on learning to negotiate.

Another place where IT leaders need to be honest and candid is with their own capabilities and weaknesses. When you're candid about your weaknesses, you can surround yourself with people who are strong in those areas. And when you take this self-assessment, it's important to identify real areas of weakness, not superficial ones. Maybe you're weak at selling ideas, overloading your schedule, getting impatient with people, or losing your temper. Maybe you have trouble developing relationships, motivating or coaching direct reports, delegating responsibility, being positive, or maybe you're shy. Once you identify such challenges, you can begin to work on them or hire people who can fill in the gaps.

Mindset Change 5: Prepare for and Embrace Change

The IT profession is all about change. And if you as an IT leader resist change or never see it coming, it can have a truly negative impact on the company and on your career. If you act like the ostrich with its head in the sand, choosing to ignore change, you'll miss the opportunity to effectively manage the expectations of the business, your clients, and your staff.

Change comes in many forms. There can be changes in corporate culture, business direction, industry competition, or in technology direction. There can be disruptions in the geographic landscape or changes to government regulations, legal requirements, and security threats.

Whatever the flavor of change, we need to be aware of its potential and be capable of analyzing how to deal with it. One good way to do that is to apply the SWOT tool—identifying the strengths, weaknesses, opportunities, and threats of the change. This topic is so strategic that Chapter 11 has been dedicated to developing the ability to lead change.

Mindset Change 6: Anticipate, Understand, Respect, and Work through Complexities

There's no getting around the fact that our success depends on our relationships with our clients, peers, and staff. Effective leaders absolutely must get out of their offices and from behind their computers and work on developing relationships. It's only by frequently talking with clients, staff, and peers that you can anticipate what's coming down the road, develop a mature understanding of how that affects key constituents, and gain the trust of the people you work with to respectfully work through those changes and complexities.

You might even consider developing a relationship strategy. At one company I consulted with, IT leaders worked to identify five or six key people they needed to develop relationships with, whether they were clients or members of the executive team. From there, they could move on to another group of people, developing relationships in a genuine, unforced manner.

Five Critical Success Factors that Enable IT Organizational Excellence

Changing your own mindset is one thing. Leading your IT organization through a successful transformation is quite another. In my work with technology leaders around the country, I've

Maximize Your Strategy, People, and Operations Investments

FIGURE 2.1 Five Critical Success Factors that Enable IT Organizational Excellence

determined that there are five challenges leaders need to work through when they want to reposition themselves and their organizations for success (see Figure 2.1).

Leadership: Lead by Positively Influencing and Inspiring Others

The exceptional technology leaders I've seen have an inner quality that makes other people want to follow them. That means learning to influence and persuade others by sharpening interpersonal skills and communication techniques. It requires building trusting relationships that enhance our ability to get things done through other people. It also requires becoming resilient as you learn ways to increase your energy and effectiveness under pressure. Building these skills is so important that they're covered in more depth in Chapter 4 on consulting skills, Chapter 5 on negotiating, and Chapter 8 on political savvy.

Strategy: Establish the Right Winning Game Plan for Your Organization

The second challenge is developing a transformation strategy for your organization to follow. A well-constructed, thorough blueprint is the first step to setting the stage for IT success. In fact, a solid game plan is essential to increasing profitability and competitive advantage, driving down expenses, maximizing productivity, strengthening customer service, optimizing people potential, and protecting client, investor, and company data.

What if you were planning to take a cross-country car trip—would you just get in the car and drive, or would you develop the best plan to get you there? Would you think you were doing well just to drive really fast, or would you want to be sure you were headed in the right direction? It's amazing that we plan our car trips better than we plan our IT activities! Remember: Activity does not equal progress. We need to develop a strategy for getting from here to there, one that works for everyone involved with the plan.

I like to think of strategy as a river, with many different tributaries feeding into it. Each tributary represents something that eventually helps build the ultimate plan, whether it's marketing the IT organization, continuously improving performance, optimizing human capital, understanding the business needs and putting together the technology architecture. We need to work on each of these building blocks to help develop a strong overall plan.

Too often, I see strategies that are so nebulous that there's nothing concrete or actionable for anyone to grab hold of. Other times, they're complex, 500-page binders that collect dust on a shelf. Still other times, I see a strategy that's well constructed but hasn't been communicated effectively. Just recently, I visited a company at which the IT leader had developed a strategy but hadn't clearly communicated it to the leadership team. When I asked them to explain their strategy, they just looked at the floor!

So, what should the strategy look like? It should be simple, no longer than a 12-page document, with some graphics that clearly display the strategy focus and the plans to make it come to fruition. And it shouldn't just sit on a shelf—strategies need to be reviewed and refreshed (although not necessarily rewritten) every three to six months because things change. It's a living, breathing document that needs to be communicated across the organization so people understand where exactly they plug in.

I advise IT leaders to communicate their strategy in many different ways, including face-to-face, formal gatherings, and informal small-group forums. I also encourage them to avoid devising unachievable or intangible targets driven by generic ideals and blue-sky thinking. Too often, I've seen IT groups discard fuzzy visions that they disdain as flavor-of-the-day management.

Strategy is also not built in a vacuum. It's vitally important to identify and involve key constituents, particularly those who will provide the business perspective. Most important, we can't let the strategy focus exclusively on technology selection.

Once the strategy is established, we can articulate and prioritize our activities. Remember, it's always better to execute on a few activities and see success rather than bite off too many things and execute poorly.

People: Hire and Professionally Develop Your Winning Team

The third challenge is to form the team who will work together to execute the strategy. I've never seen a strong leader who operated alone. Our staffs and leadership teams are our life-blood to achieving success. That's why CIOs, CTOs, and anyone in charge of an IT team also needs to learn how to select, coach, develop, and optimize their staffs.

One of the worst mistakes I see happening in IT organizations is the short-circuiting of the interview process, in which questions are superficial, and employees are hired based merely on "chemistry." Quick hiring decisions often result in the selection of the wrong person, which can lead to lost productivity, increased costs, missed performance targets, or poor employee morale. A surprising number of companies do a horrible job of checking references, even though the best predictor of future behavior is past behavior. When I've checked references, I've always gotten great information. You just have to come across as personable, professional, and willing to help out the reference should they also need anything in the future.

As leaders, we need to know how to assess who on our staffs—or from outside the organization—has the right competencies and capabilities to execute the strategy and then develop plans to help these people grow and professionally develop.

Training efforts should be aimed at the right people, taking into consideration how each employee will immediately leverage it, how it will be integrated into daily work, and how the results will be measured. We also need to retain our highest performers and develop succession plans in case a top performer leaves the company.

Strong performance measurement also comes into play, especially to measure how well the leadership team fosters a culture of collaboration among their teams. For example, how well do they support their peers? What have they done to develop genuine relationships with key stakeholders? How well are they hiring, retaining, and developing their own staffs?

When I was hired as CIO, the first thing I did was throw down the gauntlet to the leadership team and told them they'd have to break down the silos in their areas, work out the adversarial relationships that existed, and operate as a cohesive team. I made it clear that as leaders, they were responsible for sitting down together—without me as an arbitrator (we're all adults, after all) and negotiating a game plan in which the enterprise itself was the winner. I made it clear that no personal agendas were allowed—we would do what was best for the business, period. Thereafter, everyone in the organization knew we had no choice but to play well with one another. I tolerated no we-versus-them attitudes.

Breaking down these silos and rewarding teamwork and collaboration takes a great deal of work and leadership to accomplish, but it is absolutely essential. But most organizations are not structured this way—it's more often a culture of every man for himself. It looks like a bunch of people who jumped into a rowboat, started rowing in all different directions and ended up going around in circles. The fact is, we're all in the same boat, and to make any progress at all, we all have to row in the same direction. And the top IT leader is 1,000 percent responsible for that because only she can set the tone.

In summary, leaders need to do the following when it comes to hiring and professional development:

- Instill leadership competencies and behaviors
- Select people with the right skills and experiences that align with the position qualifications to execute the technology strategy
- Build leadership bench strength
- Embrace performance measurement and best practice methodologies that shape behaviors into desired results
- Learn how to select the right employees the first time
- Identify professional development programs that deliver sustainable results through phased-in learning, accountability mechanisms, and coaching

■ Recognize that employee interpersonal competency and skill development is mandatory

Best Practices: Leverage IT Best Practices Right-Sized for Your Organization

Once you've got the right people in place, it's time to start thinking about execution. But before you do that, you need to become current with the best practices in your area of focus (commonly found in the Fortune 500), select the ones that are right for your organization, and then resize them to fit your company's structure, culture, complexity, strategies, goals, and business and technology drivers. Even small- and medium-size companies can benefit from right-sizing the best practices of larger organizations.

Best practices are a fundamental cornerstone of any technology strategy. After all, why reinvent the wheel when there are time-tested, established approaches that achieve great results every time? Best practices also help us break out of the pattern of doing things the same way we've always done them.

Of course, it's also important to avoid the dangers of best practices, such as creating a highly complex, cumbersome process that kills organizational agility, stifles innovation and creativity, and destroys customer service. Best practices can't be taken off the shelf and used without customizing them to our own company culture. I always advise companies not to use anything more complex than what the situation calls for. As a great CIO I know once said, "If a client wants simple directions to the store around the corner, don't give them an elaborate map showing them how to get to the North Pole."

You also have to be careful to adopt best practices that truly match the challenges you're trying to solve, not the ones that look good because of all the buzz and hype around them. Use what makes sense for your organization and for your end goal. I see too many IT organizations apply best practices without stopping to ask, "What's the problem we're trying to solve, and what do we need to do about it?"

Done right, best practices can apply to all facets of our IT organizations, including strategy, talent, finance, operations, systems and applications development, customer relationships, third-party relationships, and communications components. Some best-practice programs include:

- Business and technology plan alignment
- Client relationship management
- Business needs assessment
- Performance scorecards and measurements
- Portfolio management
- Project management office
- Risk management
- Organization change management
- Business case development
- Selective outsourcing
- Problem and change management
- Service level management
- Financial management
- Vendor management

Execution: Translate Your Strategy, Goals, and Initiatives into Specific Action Plans that Deliver Measurable Results

The final challenge—execution—is when the real action begins. Or it's supposed to, anyway. In actuality, this is when many IT leaders drop the ball. What I find is that IT leaders regularly underestimate what's required to reach the end goal. They don't step back and look at all the moving parts and complexities, put together a game plan that addresses the top priorities, implement the mechanisms to be sure the game plan takes root, and then measure the results to ensure the end goal was achieved.

Surprisingly, many IT leaders seem to think that all they have to do is say, "We're going to go do 'X,'" and it will get done. Without a real execution plan in place, they don't realize that X will simply wither on the vine. Eventually another priority will come along—let's call it "Y"—and suddenly everyone shifts over to working on Y and abandons X until it's just another forgotten initiative.

At some companies, this happens often enough that the IT organization learns to regard new strategies as the new flavor of the day that after a bit of lip service will fizzle out. They learn to simply ignore any new initiative that comes along. At a company I was consulting with, a staffer once said to me, "There's no way this new strategy will ever happen, so I'm just going to bide my time for a few months until it goes away."

That's why I advise IT leaders to run their transformation initiatives like they would any other project, in which they assign a project manager, form project teams, develop project plans, create reporting mechanisms, and measure results. It's amazing how many organizations shudder at that thought! One client told me it's because they wanted their transformation initiative to be regarded as fun, and projects were decidedly not seen that way. I pointed out to them that you can create elements of the transformation that are fun but that on the whole, leadership work is tough. You need structure, and you need people who are committed to driving the changes into the fabric of the organization's culture.

I've seen IT leaders who simply can't do this kind of transformation work because they don't want to make unpopular decisions. They're not willing to make the choices to make the transformation work become reality. They just want to be regarded as a nice guy. But part of being a leader is making those tough decisions. And your staff will thank you for it. It's like raising kids—they'll always test the boundaries, but in the end, they operate better when they know where the boundaries are.

Execution is not a simple thing. It involves translating strategies, goals, and initiatives into action plans, project plans, and individual performance plans. You need to plan the work, empower your people, balance strategy with tactics, capture key performance indicators, track performance progress, adjust to changing conditions, measure the results, and apply lessons learned to strengthen future execution precision.

All along the way, it's vital to have the right tools in place to be sure people are executing on the work. This requires having a set of measurements and using a balanced scorecard approach, based on the results clients want to see. The whole goal is to see the project through the client's eyes and ensure you're capturing the right set of measurements from the client's perspective.

But the key word is *results*—too many times, IT organizations think things are going well when there's lots of activity. Well, it has to be the right activity, aimed at achieving the right results. Customers are mainly interested in speed, low cost, expected outcomes, and a good overall experience; high-performance organizations will deliver on all four of those components.

Conclusion: High-Performance Reality

Leadership is a journey, not a destination. IT leaders need to continually raise the bar, working relentlessly to develop themselves and their staffs to improve their leadership qualities. I've seen organizations take years to do this when they start from scratch, but I've also seen others make quantum leaps in very short periods of time because they were hungry and prepared for the change.

If developing and executing an IT transformation were easy, every IT organization would be doing it. But enduring such a change is absolutely essential to distinguishing yourself from a dying breed. IT leaders simply aren't what they used to be, and choosing complacency is like choosing to be the frog in a pot of water that's gradually being brought to a boil. If you don't want to become a casualty, you better not sit around.

We've all observed people in other industries turn a blind eye to changes that are clearly making them obsolete. Now that the spotlight is on IT, it's time to adjust your own vision and see your way to a needed transformation.

Top Ten

Leadership Strategies for Transforming Your IT Team

10. Prioritize time investment to deliver optimal results.
9. Build solid client relationships and strategies.
8. Effectively navigate politics and executive team dynamics.
7. Keep abreast of technology and business trends.
6. Think strategically while balancing tactics.
5. Align with the business.
4. Focus on results.
3. Keep promises.
2. Be resilient and effective under pressure.
1. Build trusting relationships.

Specific Actions I Will Take

-
-
-

CHAPTER 3

Building a Client-Focused
IT Culture

When you hear the term *good service*, what springs to mind? Dinner at a four-star restaurant? Flying first class? Staying at a luxury hotel? But when you think about what separates these elevated experiences from the more mundane (a rushed lunch at a diner, a middle seat on an overcrowded plane), it's not all about the imported food, the $10,000 mattress, or the extra elbow room. There's an essential ingredient that must be served alongside that free glass of champagne before you'll be satisfied, and that ingredient is called service.

But how do you define good service? At an abstract level, it's the sense that the people involved with the transaction are fully engaged with meeting the expectations you have regarding the experience they're providing. For example, the surroundings are clean and well-decorated, your needs are met promptly and courteously, you're treated with respect, and if you ask for something that's not within the usual range of offerings, the staff works to accommodate you the best it can.

Less abstractedly, it's the waiter who checks on your order even though he's not assigned to your table. It's the hotel receptionist who offers you food and beverage credits if the reservation system neglected to honor your request for a nonsmoking room. It can even be the retail clerk who looks you in the eye and asks—in a manner that suggests he truly cares about your response—whether you want to bring home your purchases in a paper or plastic bag.

Notice we've left the luxury environment at this point. Just because you expect to receive this type of service when you're paying a premium, that doesn't mean it's impossible to find four-star service at any convenience mart or roadside hotel. And just think what happens when you do encounter good service in these commodity-level places—if you later have a choice of which hotel to frequent, you'll very likely return to the one that not only rented you a room but was also engaged in the experience of bringing you satisfaction as a customer.

Now think about the characteristics of good service as it pertains to the work your own IT team does every day, maintaining, supporting, and building technology systems to enable clients to carry out business initiatives. Are downtime and upgrades planned at times that are most convenient for your clients—or for the IT organization? When a client approaches someone in the IT organization with a request, does the individual tell the client it's not their area, or does he look up the name of the person who can best help the client and then walk the client to that person's cubicle? Or when a client explains a problem to the help desk, do they get a gruff, "What operating system are you on," or a reassuring, "I'm sure we can get that resolved—why don't we start with what operating system you're running?"

From what I've seen as an internal consultant with Unisys and Canon and during my 15 years as a consultant with O&A, being a service provider is a new idea for many IT professionals. A remark I often hear from people who participate in the workshops I facilitate on this topic is, "Isn't *what* we deliver more important than *how* we deliver it?" But for anyone who feels this way, it's time to think about the job and career in a different light.

The fact is, I've watched IT leaders and staff make and break their reputations with service missteps, thinking that their client base is secure and has nowhere else to go. An even bigger fallacy that I've witnessed is the belief that if the outcome of the work is good, it doesn't matter how difficult you were to work with. As a result, IT is unappreciated and undervalued and seemingly blind to the minor (and major) service irritants that trip up their reputations.

To me, it's an absolute shame that many of the smartest, hardest working, and logical members of any company are so unappreciated and undervalued. It's imperative that understanding IT's role as a service provider (not servant!) is essential to IT getting to the table and being heard as a true and valued partner.

Because whether your staff believes it or not, the best way to build client loyalty is not by proving IT's technology prowess but by building a service strategy that enables internal IT to be seen as a top provider of service. In fact, a well-developed and well-communicated service strategy is critical in today's IT organizations. Clients demand service to be immediate and proactive, and if they don't get it internally, they'll find it, either by hiring their own staff or external vendors. Indeed, good service is no longer just a nice-to-have; it's the make-or-break factor that determines whether clients choose internal IT or someone else to deliver the solutions they need.

In too many IT organizations that I encounter, a good service strategy means "being all things to all people." But while everyone is equal in the eyes of the U.S. Constitution, not everyone is equal from a service perspective. In others, the service strategy seems to be to provide service only to the people who scream the loudest and have the most clout. This leads to a tremendous amount of frustration on the part of IT, as well as the clients who don't have that same level of clout.

I also see IT organizations that have created service strategies that are interwoven with their governance practices, where a committee makes decisions about what's best for the organization at large. This strategy can be great, but I notice a lot of confusion both among the business community and the IT staff about how this strategy actually operates. That's usually because this strategy requires lots of communication as to how decisions are made, especially since the lag time between meetings can be months.

But most of the time, I see no strategy at all, or even well-thought-out strategies that haven't been communicated well to those providing the service. Having a clear communication plan is the key.

For all of these reasons, the development of a service strategy has to start at the top of the IT organization—with the IT leader. These strategies require cultivation and have to be planned and led by the IT leadership team. The strategy has to be consistent across the enterprise, and it must permeate every project, not be something that "only Joe" provides. After all, good service is not defined by good relationships with individual clients. The purpose is to look out for the enterprise, not to make "my friend in accounting" happy.

At its best, service is a mentality, an attitude, a glue that holds together the entire department. And it can't spring from a negative environment. The turnaround can be difficult, and it can be costly, but it can also turn your internal IT group into a must-have resource for clients.

What Good Service Looks Like

Let's start by talking about what service doesn't look like. Number one, service is not subservience. It's not about becoming submissive order takers who deliver anything the client desires. But while IT can't do everything the client asks for, it can convey a willingness to serve, and it does this by addressing the client's needs with respect and concern. If you've succeeded, the client walks away from the transaction, thinking, "I really like working with these people."

Service also can't spring from a negative atmosphere. Unfortunately, many IT departments are hotbeds of negativity. I hear IT professionals complain about feeling unappreciated, angry, and victimized. "We're always called in at the last minute," is a frequent comment, or, "All the decisions are already made by the business," or, "We're invited to the party after all the food is gone." In other cases, I detect a note of arrogance—"They couldn't survive a day without us," or, "It's always up to us to save their skins."

No wonder when some IT leaders ask their staff to up their service game, they might glumly play a role that they think looks like good service but isn't. It's the mentality of the store checkout clerk who asks without expression or eye contact whether we found everything okay or the false smile of the flight attendant who tells us to have a good day. If there's one thing about good service, it only passes the sniff test when it's sincere.

So what does good service look like from an IT point of view? Some characteristics include:

- Sincerity
- Righting wrongs instead of abdicating responsibility
- Addressing issues promptly and courteously
- Working to understand the client's needs
- Going out of your way to resolve an issue
- Being easy to work with
- Approaching issues constructively

Above all, service starts with understanding—and really caring about—the client's goals and concerns. This requires a change of attitude, from negative to positive, and to thinking of the client's concerns as imperative to IT's function, not something that gets in the way. Sometimes it's easiest to convey what this change of mindset looks like by showing some examples:

- Instead of listing all the reasons IT can't support something, how about listing what the organization can support that might meet the need? (Of course, that involves asking what the client's need is in the first place.)
- Instead of telling clients that the changes they're requesting will throw the project off budget and off schedule, how about laying out the impacts and asking what's most important to the client?
- When a server goes down or the client isn't able to access a particular application, how about an apology for the impact to her job?
- How about telling clients that you're thinking about them and their business, for example, by sending them a note of congratulations when they win a large project or finish something for the company?

In my workshops, I also like to point out the two most common wrongdoings I see committed in IT today when the subject comes to service, as well as how to correct them. These two service sins happen when people play the roles of either the Rule Master or the Promiser. The Rule Master says things like, "That's not part of the project plan," or "That's not our company standard," or, "We don't do it that way," or, "That's not our policy."

On the other hand, the Promiser just says, "Yes." "We can do that," "We can do that too," and, "Is there anything else you want us to do?"

Both roles are played with the best of intentions—the Rule Master's is to manage expectations and protect the company, while the Promiser's is to build good relationships. The best way to stop these common practices is by taking those best intentions and getting them pointed in the right direction.

For example, with the Rule Master, hold a staff meeting and ask your team what rules they're most often asked to break. You'll likely hear things like, circumventing the process, starting work without funding or approval, giving access rights to unauthorized individuals, providing support for clients' home devices. Then, as a team, discuss what your reply should be to each one. The reply should focus on what IT can do to help or better understand the root problem the client needs help with.

And if there's a rule that clients continuously challenge, that gives you two pieces of information. First, maybe it's time to get rid of this rule. If not, maybe it's time to address this rule at a communication level, so everyone understands the business rationale behind it. Again, as leaders, we must make sure we're not giving exceptions to the rules simply because it's uncomfortable.

With the Promiser role, it's important to understand that saying yes makes everyone happy at first, but if you can't deliver on that yes, it's the disappointment and anger that will be remembered. So, first IT needs to understand what situations cause them to overpromise. Second, you need to plan some phrases that show your concern, prove you're knowledgeable, and that give you a chance to truly listen and understand before committing to anything. For example, you might say, "I know you're asking us for a delivery date, as this change is really important to you. But given that importance, we want to make sure we can commit to the date so that you're pleased at the end of the project and not just now. Let's keep talking about what you need and then give us a half-day to get back to you with a commitment."

If the meeting is virtual, having a signal or key word can help each other understand when someone has begun to overcommit.

Service Skills and Mindsets

IT leaders need to help all members of the IT staff develop a new mindset to help them transition their organizations to a service-oriented culture. Here are three skills I teach in my workshop to evolve participants' mindset toward a service-oriented culture.

A *We* Mindset

Developing a service mentality is not an individual effort. It's a team sport, where things like a good pass, an assist, or runs batted in are more important than achieving a personal best. In other words, think football, basketball, and baseball, not golf, track, or swimming. A superstar is always fun to watch, but the more the team depends solely on that player's performance, the less chance it has of winning.

The we mentality is important on many levels. The first is within the IT team itself. All too often, people in the IT department take one another for granted, treating each other as though they don't count as much as other coworkers do. But imagine what the IT group would look like if its members saw one another as deserving of a prescribed level of service. Not only would group members work together in a more fluid, respectful, and effective way, but also good intradepartment service is essential for providing good service outward, to business clients. If there's negativity within the IT organization itself, it will surely be evident to the business community.

The team mentality is also important because a service-oriented culture requires that clients experience consistency across all members of the IT team. In other words, no matter which individual a client works with, he or she needs to experience the same positive attitude. If some team members are friendly and engaged while others are angry and negative, clients will simply avoid the unpleasant individuals and seek out the constructive ones. At one health organization I worked with, clients regularly avoided asking for help on the days when they knew a particular IT professional was assigned to help them.

Consistency is important for another reason—developing loyalty among business clients. Imagine you're taking a road trip on which you'll need to make a couple of overnight stops before reaching your destination. At your most road-weary, you pull into the parking lot of a brand-name hotel, where in the past you learned to expect a certain level of service. You expect to park close to the hotel door, walk into a clean lobby, easily get a room that meets your needs, take a swim in an attractive pool, get a simple dinner at a nearby restaurant, and sleep in a comfortable bed.

Now, what would happen if the brand-name hotel you chose didn't meet those expectations? What if the staff never brought the extra towels you requested, the receptionist couldn't recommend a good family restaurant, and no one was available to make more coffee at the free breakfast buffet? As you grumpily drove off after such a poor-quality experience, would you choose that brand of hotel at the next stop? It would help if the low service level was an anomaly, but at the very least, it would reduce your enthusiasm for using that brand again.

Similarly, clients will more quickly increase their loyalty to internal IT when each and every experience they have with IT team members is a positive one. It's an unfortunate fact that negative experiences have much more impact than positive ones.

A we attitude is also important when it comes to the IT organization's relationship with its clients. Too often, IT develops an us versus them mentality toward the business, which suggests a separation at best and a combative relationship at worst. To shift toward a service-oriented culture, that us versus them gap must be closed. IT organizations must realize that they and the business are part of the same whole, that the very reason they want to provide excellent service is that they're working with their business counterparts together to achieve common organizational goals.

At one company, this destructive mentality was so strong that the IT group had started a Stupid User award at their monthly staff meeting, when they'd vote on the stupidest thing a user had done that month. While there's nothing wrong with blowing off some steam, institutionalizing and emphasizing such a superior attitude was not going to help this group develop a service mentality. When they realized this, the group turned the award around, voting instead on the smartest thing they'd noticed a user doing that month.

This us versus them mentality can also creep in when IT professionals mistakenly interpret the service provider role to be that of an order taker. If you can picture yourself pulling out an order pad and taking down requirements without understanding what the client wants and why, you need to stop what you're doing and get engaged. Internal IT and the business client are both part of the same community that has a vested interested in doing the best job for the company, and there's no room for us versus them; there's only room for *we*.

Learning to Love Complaints

This is one of the harder mindsets to develop. Who could love a complaint, whether it's in the form of a neighbor who can't stand your dog barking or a threatening letter from the bank? Well, what if you stripped the emotion out of the complaints you hear and simply saw them as input or information that you otherwise wouldn't be privy to? Don't you want to know that your dog barks for an hour as soon as you leave the house? Or, that your check bounced? If you didn't hear the complaint, how else would you be able to take action before something worse happened?

IT needs to learn to love comments like, "What were you people thinking when you chose this standard?" "Will you ever accomplish anything on time?" "I like you, but that other group in IT, the business analysts, they're very arrogant." "You know we call it the help-less desk, don't you?" "It's been two months since I put in that request. How come I can track my package with UPS but you folks manage to lose things?"

The IT organization needs to know that its standard hasn't been well received or well communicated. It needs to know that a peer group has an arrogant reputation (and so do they)! It needs to know the help desk hasn't been given the tools that they need to properly help callers. It needs to know that somehow a request has been neglected.

As an IT professional, it should be much more disconcerting to *not* hear your clients complaining—all too often, unhappy clients remain quiet, giving you no chance to prove you can do better. And bad news does have a way of spreading more quickly than good news. For better or worse, complaints are often your clients' form of communication, and not only should you treasure them, but you should also encourage them. Complaints are a learning opportunity, your opportunity to get it right. You can't do something with what you don't know.

In some ways, complaints are comparable to the problems IT works on every day. What's often missing is the process of resolving them. Unlike a system glitch—which gets tracked, trended, and reported on—you may not know what to do with a complaint. That's what makes it so crucial to harness complaints and address them through a complaint management process. If complaints are addressed quickly, courteously, and effectively, imagine the percentage of the complainers who will come back to you with their future needs.

But first you have to interpret complaints correctly, which means listening for the problem being expressed. This isn't always easy. Complaints often sound disrespectful, or even hostile. But as soon as you look beyond the personal dig and turn complaints into something that's trackable, logical, nonpersonal, and unemotional, they're easier to deal with. That means overcoming IT's natural defensiveness—"Technology changes overnight; we're lucky we can keep up with it," "You think you've got problems?" Or even a tendency to agree in nonconstructive ways—"Yeah, I know, the situation really stinks," or "Yes, our policies really are archaic." What message gets sent with those responses?

IT organizations need to develop a new way of responding, which most people aren't trained to do. A workable process might look like this.

> *Step 1:* Thank the client for making the complaint. It sounds counterintuitive, but this step really helps to force a mindset change. A simple, "Thank you for letting us know" will do, and you might even want to add a little marketing twist: "It wasn't our intention to make the process seem slow."
>
> *Step 2:* Gather more information. You need to help your staff get past defensiveness and start asking questions to find out more about the problem. Make sure their line of questioning is open-ended and designed to let the client tell his side of the events. The goal is to investigate, not interrogate. The attitude should be, "Tell me what's wrong; how did it happen; how can I better understand the situation?"
>
> *Step 3:* Apologize for the circumstances. Even if you don't think it was IT's fault, you can express this as, "It wasn't our intention to interrupt your business process," or "I'm very sorry you had that experience."
>
> *Step 4:* Ask how you can help. This doesn't mean pulling out the order-taker pad or putting on your "I'll-fix-everything" hat. This step requires really listening to all the circumstances of what happened and what the client is unhappy about and coming away with a commitment to taking measures that rectify the situation.

It's all too easy to cut the conversation short and ask the client to send an e-mail, detailing the complaint. But it's crucial to take the time to follow these four steps when the client is in front of us, willing to talk. And it's just as crucial that when the conversation ends, the client feels a commitment has been made to resolve the problem to her full satisfaction.

Note that resolution and satisfaction don't always mean making the client happy. For example, if someone complained that the company wasn't moving more quickly toward a new computing platform, you can't snap your fingers and make the budget appear to do that. However, you can ask the client to flesh out his concerns and ask how you can help him feel more comfortable with the pace of new technology adoption. Maybe you can share the schedule of when the new platform will be adopted, as well as your thoughts on why it's smart to hold out for that time frame.

Again, the *how* is just as important as the *what*—and that includes the tone and manner in which you communicate. Even if it feels like you've addressed the same complaint a dozen times that day, you need to avoid sounding like you'd really just like the client to go away. When IT professionals start to feel like their jobs would be so much better if their clients would just leave them alone, that's when you know you're heading down the wrong path. Because the result might be exactly along those lines—the clients will indeed leave you alone, as they make their arrangements with a new technology provider.

And none of this is easy to do when emotions are high. At one hospital I worked with, the IT group had taken down the pharmacy system over the weekend for maintenance, without warning the people who depended on it 24×7. On Monday morning, when they walked in to irate clients, it was hard for the group to not feel completely discouraged. But because of their progress toward incorporating a service-oriented mentality, they were able to turn that attitude around to realize that through the mistake, they learned valuable lessons. They thanked the clients for detailing their complaints, ensured them of their commitment to rectify the situation, and were able to move on. Through their service mentality, they gained an opportunity to recover from a bad situation.

Making Every Interaction Count

The third mindset focuses on the daily interactions IT has with its clients (both business clients and IT peers) and recognizing that every impression counts when it comes to providing good service. I call these *moments of truth*—interactions that leave our clients with an impression of IT's performance, whether positive or negative. The term *moments of truth* was conceptualized in 1984 by service management guru Richard Normann and later popularized by Jan Carlzon, a renowned business leader and turnaround specialist, who wrote a book by that title.

In the average IT organization, hundreds or thousands of these moments of truth occur every day. Clients form impressions every time they encounter the IT group, from the first voice they hear when calling the help desk, to the first link they click on IT's web site, to the first person they see when they enter the IT group's area of the building or campus.

Moments of truth can work to IT's benefit or detriment. While one negative experience can cause the client's impression to sour, it takes just one positive interaction to begin repairing a negative experience. If you map out the service you provide into moments of truth, you can start to understand how clients experience the internal IT group and start making micro-improvements that can have a huge impact.

Consider what happens when a business department becomes interested in off-the-shelf software it can use to help it better communicate with the company's suppliers. The client talks to the vendor, and in doing so, experiences the following moments of truth: The vendor compliments the client, tells them he's ahead of the game, gives him a demo showing all the great things this product can do for the organization, leaves behind a good-looking brochure, and provides an estimate within the promised week.

Then the client talks to internal IT. In this case, the moments of truth can go one of two ways. In the first, IT reacts positively, saying, "Yes, we've heard about this product, and we'd love to sit down and hear your goals for what it can do for you." IT then compliments the client for their savviness in the technical area (only if it's true, of course) and promises to provide an estimate within the week. In the other scenario, IT could tell the client it has too many projects going on right now to deal with the client's request. IT then tells the client it can't even research the system until it assigns a project or task number and ends the conversation with a noncommittal, "We'll get back to you."

Notice that I haven't even begun talking about the moments of truth involved with refining requirements, testing, going live, and support. Each of these stages can have hundreds of moments of truth, involving different clients who are part of that same organization.

Consider the moments of truth involved when IT sends out an e-mail announcing it needs to perform a system upgrade. Moments of truth can include: Who the e-mail is from? What's in the subject line? What does this mean to me? When will this occur? Can I opt out of this? If the upgrade involves turning in a laptop or PDA for a new, better one, moments of truth can include: What does the device look like? Is all my old stuff on it? What has been removed? What does the new device look like? What has been added? Where is that certain function I like? How long is this going to take? Can I reschedule? Then the client needs to figure out how to be productive again. Here, moments of truth include: Did this technology actually improve my work, and when I call for support, is the staff knowledgeable, or were they just trying to get up to speed on it themselves?

When you have virtual clients, moments of truth are a bit more challenging to manage. First, these clients expect a quick reply to their calls, e-mails, or instant messages, just as nonvirtual clients do. If the staff isn't available during certain hours, expectations need to be managed through out-of-office features on e-mail and through updated voice mail announcements. Second, because it can be easy to lose touch with virtual clients, you need to make sure your top ten clients are contacted by phone at least once per month. Third, it's also easy to lose track of how changes in the home office affect virtual clients. This boils down to more communication by IT regarding the changes that affect these clients.

Moments of truth can also be less formalized, like interactions with clients we pass in the hallway. If someone stops to give an IT staffer her idea for a new enhancement to an application, does the staff person look the client in the eye? How does he react—with a sarcastic, "Great, another new idea," or with a positive, "Those are the kinds of suggestions we're always looking for." Even nonverbal reactions count, including facial expressions, eye contact, and tone. All of these leave long-lasting impressions.

Remember, attitude is everything. Does your staff turn requirements-gathering meetings into grill sessions, or are they enthusiastically engaged in the discussion? These are all the ways in which clients measure the IT organization.

If you map out all the moments of truth that clients experience with the IT organization and assess what their experience is like through those interactions, you'll have a good idea of your organization's level of service and where it needs to improve. This can range from voice tone and body language to a grander scale, like revamping all your forms or streamlining your web interface.

Strategies for Developing a Service Mentality

At any point in time, an individual IT professional can decide to change her own approach to providing service—whether by adopting new body language or tone of voice or even the way

FIGURE 3.1 The Service Strategy Cycle

she responds to client complaints. However, the real call to action is for the entire IT department to undergo a cultural shift (see Figure 3.1). It's up to the IT leader to not only acknowledge that it's crucial to craft a service strategy, but to also communicate the strategy and be sure it's used consistently by all members of the IT staff. Here are some tips for making a service strategy work.

Never Let It Go

IT leaders who want to affect a service mentality culture talk about the issue all the time. At every meeting, no matter how technical, they convey the sense that the client is at the center of the discussion, or they make the connection between how the technology issues intertwine with the business. One company that had traditionally incorporated a safety moment into every monthly meeting, when the IT group discussed one thing it had done to improve its alignment with OSHA standards, also began incorporating a customer service moment, when it reported on measures taken to better serve customers.

IT leaders also need to encourage individuals to understand what their clients are working on, what the business is doing, and what the stress points are. This can be done quite easily through many tools that most companies already offer, such as internal newsletters and web sites that many people in IT may not think to read. It doesn't need to be time consuming; skimming through the information or just looking at the table of contents can yield valuable insights.

Another way to conquer the time commitment conundrum is to take a divide-and-conquer approach. For example, I've seen some companies assign various IT team members to read business journals or books pertaining to the company's industry and make a 30-minute presentation on what they learned at a monthly meeting. The same idea could be applied to field trips into the various client areas that IT serves, whether it's the manufacturing line, the reservation system, or the marketing area.

It's surprisingly easy to forget about making clients the center of your everyday life. At one think-tank organization, the CIO got so wrapped up in managing budgets, reorganizations, internal staff, and meetings that he realized one day that it had been two years since he'd last talked with any of the IT department's clients. He certainly wasn't shirking his job; he simply lost sight of the attitude that anything the group was doing was for the sake of the client.

A challenge we frequently hear is that while individual leaders within the organization get it in terms of having and conveying a service mentality, other leaders don't and actually do harm. While this can be very discouraging, it's all about perseverance. Those of us who do get it need to continue reminding our peers about the impact we have on determining IT's reputation. Research shows that peer pressure works well in changing others' behavior. So the best you can do to influence other IT leaders throughout the organization is to continue reminding them of the importance of a service mentality and initiating small steps, such as the ones mentioned in this chapter to show your commitment and stay positive. Make it a mental game if necessary.

Clearly Define Your Service Level Offerings

With compressed budgets and time schedules, the days are gone when IT can or even should offer the same level of service to all of its clients or even assign the same service level to all areas of IT. It's more strategic to define several levels of service and decide how to apply those levels based on the needs of your clients.

For example, you might define three levels of service:

1. *Basic:* Focus on quick turnaround
2. *Enhanced:* Focus on quick turnaround and client convenience
3. *Premium:* Focus on all of the preceding plus anything else that's required, as long as the client is willing and able to pay for it

Note that all three levels are quality offerings. What changes is the amount of time that IT dedicates to the issue. For example, a client that's launching a new product that's critical to the bottom line would require premium levels of service, as would an executive traveling overseas to make an important presentation. On the other hand, a nonrevenue-producing group might be assigned basic service and be given a lot of self-service tools.

You might also expect different levels of service from different areas of IT. The help desk might be considered a basic service, where the attention is on quick turnaround, whereas technology R&D is an enhanced service that has the added requirement of hosting a web site on its findings.

No matter how many levels of service a company defines and how it applies them, it's crucial for individual team members to move easily between the various levels. It's equally important for clients to know what to expect. Retailers do a good job in this respect. Think of what you expect when you walk into a store like Nordstrom's versus Costco. Shoppers would be incensed about waiting in line at the former, but they're mentally prepared for that at Costco. A service motto can go a long way toward helping avoid the guesswork of what service clients should expect and what IT is required to give them.

The big secret to managing expectations is the ability to understand what the client's expectation is in the first place. That might sound really obvious, but IT organizations are often afraid to ask this question, because they're concerned they won't meet it. However, it's impossible to meet an expectation that's unknown.

After understanding the client's expectations, the next step is to stop focusing on what you can't do and gear your mind to what you can do. Say a client asks you to install some nonstandard software. You can't do that, but you can offer to load and support the approved standard. If clients are complaining about a late rollout, a positive response would be, "I'd be happy to call our R&D folks and find out where we are on testing this product and give you a status update on when the rollout will be." If someone asks you to change a spec on a project you're in the middle of, say, "We'd love to make that change for you, but of course, every change has an impact on the schedule or the cost. Would you like me to get those numbers for you?"

There seems to be an awkwardness (almost an embarrassment) when IT manages expectations. However, I like to remind people I work with that clients are very used to this behavior from external vendors!

Engage Your Clients in the Culture Shift

A service strategy will only be successful if your staff sees things through the eyes of the client. A great way to provide your organization with that vision is to invite clients into the process. You can ask them to share their impressions of IT service, for example, or even attend a workshop together. Some of the participants in my workshops have invited key clients to attend with them. In either case, a face-to-face dialogue is much more revealing than a written survey.

Depending on your relationship with the client, this can be a painful but eye-opening experience. For example, one manufacturer that had what it described as a broken relationship between the business and IT attended one of my workshops. A top business client frankly detailed his group's impressions of IT, many of which were negative. The revelations ranged from "We don't hear from you," to "We don't know what you're working on," to "You're always having these big reorganizations," to "When we call you, it takes you forever to respond." The message: We're in the dark, and when we need you, we can't find you.

It wasn't easy to hear, but by the end of the day, while the relationship was by no means completely mended, it was on its way to being repaired. On IT's side, this was no time to be defensive; it was time to be quiet and listen. And on the client's side, it was not so much about blame as investing the time and passion to reveal some difficult truths. In the end, it's far better for IT to hear these assessments than for the client to share them with someone else.

Conclusion

Management fads come and go, but a service-oriented mentality is no blip on the screen. It requires leadership to affect culture change from the top down, and it requires every member of the IT team to become engaged in a new mentality of delivering technology services.

Furthermore, developing a service strategy is a process, not an end result. With every day, every moment, every interaction clients have with IT, impressions are formed, for better or worse. Customer satisfaction surveys are great, but it would be wrong to focus solely on increasing your score each year. The true goal is to satisfy clients every time you interact with them.

So what do we get for providing good service? The sad fact is, there's often no immediate reward. Good service is expected; it's poor service that gets noticed. But, even if IT doesn't get credit, good service is long, long remembered, and those memories come back to benefit IT in the form of client loyalty. So when it comes time to decide between internal IT and another technology provider, it's service that will raise your IT department above commodity status.

It's important to remember that internal IT is no longer the only game in town, and the days are gone when clients depended solely on IT to provide technology services. There are other ways for clients to fulfill their technology needs, and service is a competitive part of the equation in determining which provider to use—internal or external IT.

But there is great hope here! Behaviors such as loving complaints (rather than arguing why you're right), understanding the organization and its goals, and watching the attitude of, "that's against policy" can lead to enormous goodwill from clients and allow IT to actually get credit for their phenomenal work.

If you live each day of your work life knowing it can all be taken away by an external vendor in a heartbeat, that would be the beginning of a shift toward the mentality and motivation needed to redefine your IT organization as a provider not of technology but of service.

Top Ten

Ways to Build a Client-Focused IT Culture

10. Identify and avoid the service sins you commit when under pressure.
9. Document who your clients are, as well as which services you provide to them.

8. Define the levels of service you are willing and able to provide.

7. Elicit feedback on the levels of service you choose to provide.

6. Clarify problems *before* you start fixing them.

5. Know what your clients' expectations are *before* trying to meet them.

4. Learn something new about one of your clients (goals, hot buttons, concerns).

3. If the service you provide is virtual, spend more time thinking about and creating touch points (web sites, voice mail boxes) than if you were onsite.

2. Ask clients for feedback on one self-service tool (or try it out yourself).

1. Talk to a client and ask, "What is your biggest frustration with IT?" "What is the best thing IT does?"

Specific Actions I Will Take

-
-
-

CHAPTER 4

Evolving into the Role of Consultant

Throughout life, people face big decisions that are outside their usual realm of expertise—how to pay for their kids' schooling, where to buy a house, which medical procedure is best for addressing a health concern. At those times, many of us reach out to someone with more knowledge than we have, whether it's a financial planner, a Realtor, or a doctor.

Think of the qualities you look for in the person you ultimately want to engage with: Expertise, certainly, but you might also want someone who really listens, who takes the time to understand your desires, concerns, and goals who can explain things in a way you understand and whom you can trust to have your best interests in mind.

What you're looking for is a consultant, someone with whom you can enter into a partnership that allows you to enrich your own perspective with his experience. It would be foolish to try to embark on really complex and important decisions or projects without the help of such a person.

My 25 years of experience in consulting with and for organizations has shown that unfortunately, that's not what happens in corporate America every day when the time comes to make important technology investments. When business departments embark on new strategies or seek better ways of doing their jobs, they almost always require technology expertise to reach those goals. But to whom do they turn for that expertise? Time and time again, across every industry I've consulted in, I've seen them seek out an outside consultant, a technology vendor, or a power user in the department who knows enough to be dangerous. But who ultimately needs to implement the solution? The internal IT department—often when it's so far down the road in the decision-making process that the system is difficult or even impossible to implement in a satisfactory way, given the current infrastructure and architecture of existing systems.

And after too many project failures, some business departments end up sidestepping the IT department all together. And how dysfunctional is that? It's like trying to build a house and avoiding contact with the general contractor.

In some cases, I've seen business departments enlist the help of IT earlier in the game, but with the expectation that their system specifications will be carried out without discussion or costly involvement of their staff. IT obliges, and when the system ultimately doesn't do what the client really needs it to do, everyone starts blaming one another and the system falls into disuse.

In fact, this is the situation that most resonates in the workshops I facilitate for O&A on consulting skills. One of the biggest complaints I hear from IT professionals is that they can't get their clients intimately involved in the project because they lack availability or sometimes even interest. For me, this is a clear indicator that the client is not fully owning the outcome, and that doesn't make sense, given that it's rare for any project to be an IT project—rather, it needs to be a business project.

Consider this scenario. When a Minnesota couple needed to transfer to Florida, they faxed their home requirements to a Florida Realtor. The Realtor called back and suggested a phone conference. The couple was annoyed; why couldn't the Realtor just work with their specifications? But by the end of the conversation, they learned how much they didn't know about housing in the South. In fact, had the Realtor delivered on what they'd asked for, they would have ended up with terrible buyer's remorse. In the end, they bought something they never would have considered if they hadn't engaged in the consultation—but that was ultimately the right house for them.

The lesson for IT leaders is this: Clients of computer technology are a lot like that relocating couple and like anyone who needs to get something done that's beyond their realm of expertise. We think we know what we want—a college education, a dream house, a clean bill of health—but if a trusted and learned partner doesn't help influence our decision making, we may very well end up dissatisfied. In the same way, your clients may think they know what they want, but too often what they want doesn't jibe with the reality of how technology actually works, or with existing architectures or in tandem with other systems.

In my consulting career, I've always been intrigued by what it takes to manage the dynamic forces of people, processes, and technology to create business solutions. In fact, my interest led me to pursue a master's degree in organizational development so I could better understand the human side of getting work done. Then, over the years as both an internal and external consultant, I started to recognize that the IT organization's success in bringing business solutions to fruition often came down to its ability to *influence without direct power.* And that's why today, I find great satisfaction in working with IT professionals to support their own development as internal consultants. I strongly believe that their effectiveness in partnering with the business is directly correlated with the development of their personal interaction skills.

I also believe it's crucial for IT leaders to enable themselves and their organizations to engage clients in a trusted partnership, shifting their role from order taker or technology wizard or even naysayer or bottleneck to the role of problem-solving

partner. By operating as a consultant to the business department, IT professionals and their clients are putting their capabilities together to build an optimum solution with which both sides
are happy.

What Exactly Is a Consultant's Role, Anyway?

Many IT professionals have probably never really thought about
what the word *consultant* means, and if they have, it's usually
based on a negative stereotype they have of external consultants.
But in fact, from the CIO down to entry-level staff members, everyone in the IT organization needs to expand her influence by operating as a consultant. So, let's get past the negative connotations
and think about what a consultant really is—someone who has no
direct authority or power over the people she works with but instead uses influence to guide their decisions and actions. In other
words, since consultants don't operate from a position of authority, they have to operate from a position of trust—trust not only in
their expertise but also in their ability to share that expertise in a
meaningful and applicable way with their clients.

This is true for everyone in IT, not just people with the word
consultant in their title, and not just for client-facing positions.
After all, the minute the CIO walks out of her office and into the
business community, she has lost all of her positional power and
is only as good as her ability to influence her peers and clients.
Today's reality is that the success of the IT professional absolutely hinges on earning the trust of our clients. Otherwise, why
would they listen to us?

Perhaps it's easier to understand the consultant role by envi-
sioning what it is *not*. Consultants are not the gurus at the top of
the mountain, to whom clients make pilgrimages and pay hom-
age. They are on the ground, side-by-side with the client—an
ally who is fully engaged with the business needs at hand.

Imagine a patron walking into a restaurant—he's hungry but not sure what to eat, so he asks the cook to just make him something delicious. Forty-five minutes pass, and the diner's annoyance turns to outrage when the meal finally arrives, and it's a casserole containing all sorts of vegetables that he doesn't like, sausage—which he doesn't eat—all swimming in a tomato-based sauce—and he hates tomatoes! How could his request for "something delicious" have gone so wrong? The customer sends it back, only to anger the cook, who had labored over this meal, imagining that it would send the diner into epicurean ecstasy.

Have you ever experienced that type of frustration? Like when you've agreed to insert yet another requirement into a system that's already behind schedule, only to have the client berate you a short time later when a deliverable isn't met?

Now imagine that the cook had asked the diner a few questions, like whether he's allergic to any foods, what else he'd eaten that day, whether he prefers seafood or red meat, how much he wants to spend, or whether he's ever tried parsnips before. As the cook engages the diner more fully and gains a stronger understanding of his preferences, he might steer the customer away from the dinner menu and suggest something from the luncheon menu, which can be prepared more quickly.

Just as important, the cook doesn't make the customer feel stupid when he needs to explain why it's impossible to prepare potatoes au gratin without adding cheese or why the diner probably shouldn't order a soufflé for takeout. He also doesn't waste the diner's time explaining which cooking implements he'll use, what the optimal food temperatures would be, or whether he prefers to brown the meat before roasting it. And if anything happens during the meal preparation to change the discussed outcome, he'll make sure the customer is quickly made aware of it.

Although all of this front-end work takes time, it's worth it. While awaiting his food, the customer is well prepared for what he's going to get. And when the meal arrives, he's not only completely satisfied, but he also vows to return to this restaurant because he's developed a real rapport with the cook.

That's the type of trusting relationship IT leaders need to develop with their business clients. In this type of true partnership, you're not blindly following orders or bluntly saying, "No, that can't be done" without discussing alternatives. When there's trust and real effort put into understanding the needs at hand, both the IT professional and the client can discuss, negotiate, push back, give in—all without feeling like someone needs to win or lose. Because suddenly, it's not a battle anymore.

So how do you get there? It requires IT leaders to develop a whole new mindset, as well as a set of skills to help clients define what they really need, within the constraints of budget, schedule, and what's technologically feasible. When IT organizations do this, I've seen them transform from the people called in at the last minute to the go-to group that business clients call as soon as they consider a new system need. Just like they would with a trusted consultant.

Here, generally, are the characteristics that clients expect to see in a consultant:

- Confidence in her own capabilities without arrogance
- Enthusiasm and complete engagement during the project
- Accessibility and responsiveness
- Knowledge about the client's line of business and a willingness to learn more
- Dedication to the client's best interests

Why Do I Need to Become More Consultative?

Some people ask me whether it's truly vital for IT professionals to develop their consulting skills. Isn't it more important to keep up to date with certifications and technology skills, they ask? I respond by reminding them that it's not about *either/or* but *rather/and*. As a good consultant, you need to bring value to the table. That means you bring technological perspective in respect to the business *and* you have the human interaction skills so that people will actually be able to hear what you have to say.

Over the years, I've had many IT professionals confess to me that they were resistant to this touchy-feely stuff until they tried it and evolved into a consultant role. When they do, it represents a major shift in their thinking. In fact, many will confide that they wish they'd been a little wiser much earlier in their career.

That's because in the past decade, information technology has become so intertwined with business strategy that the one can't—or shouldn't—be pursued without the other. IT professionals who are more excited about technology than its application to business initiatives will increasingly find themselves working on nonstrategic, noncore, and ultimately not very exciting projects—if they continue to be employed at all.

In my work with a major retailer, I had one of the senior business sponsors announce to a new group of IT staff members, "I get really nervous when someone from IT comes in and says, 'I have a great idea!' because I get the feeling they're probably excited about some new technology advancement. But when they come in and say they have an idea on how we can accomplish some business goal or objective—I'm all ears. I need people who are committed to helping me drive the business agenda—not the latest and greatest technology."

IT is under increased pressure to deliver technology solutions more quickly and cost effectively and to quantify the return on investment. How better to accomplish that than to pair technology projects so closely with client needs that no one could question whether any given technology project is bringing value? And how better to reduce costs than to deliver what clients really need the first time, rather than abandoning expensive efforts and going back to the drawing board time and time again? The only way to do that is to foster the relationships that enable understanding and collaboration.

Lastly, competition has never been hotter for internal IT, particularly as lower-cost offshore options are becoming a more familiar and often-used choice for low-level coding and routine testing and increasingly even more strategic projects. As one IT executive said to me recently, "I'd have my head in the sand if I didn't realize the competition is out there." Today's IT department also functions as the resource broker or the general contractor on key projects. It is their role to find the right mix of employees and onshore and offshore resources. By operating as internal consultants, the IT organization can avoid being replaced by outsourcers.

Learning to Change Hats: The Four Roles of IT

In my workshop, I refer to four different consulting roles: technical wizard, technical assistant, silent influencer, and problem-solving partner. All have intrinsic value when used at the right time. Here's a quick description of each:

1. The *Technical Wizard* is the *hero* role. They descend upon a problem with all their wizardry and save the day. You need heroes on your team, especially when there is a crisis. However, the Technical Wizard doesn't necessarily help build a shared understanding or commitment for the long term. Some clients would love nothing more than to let IT take charge with no involvement and then blame IT when it doesn't address the real need.

2. The *Technical Assistant* can appear as the *order taker*. The business department knows—or seems to know—exactly what it wants, and IT carries out the stated requirements. However, sometimes taking the order is not the right

solution. This role can result in clients getting what they ask for, but not always what they need. Their requests are not informed by the realities of what it takes to fulfill them, and IT doesn't truly understand the business situation in which the client is operating.

3. *Silent Influencers* are not actually silent but informally influence their clients' perspectives. For example, you can send clients articles on relevant topics or hold brown-bag lunch gatherings to explain technology concepts and how they relate to current business needs. You can even just check in with clients by phone or e-mail to see how things are going with existing business initiatives or ongoing projects. In some organizations, I've found this to be one of the most effective roles to gain greater ownership and in-depth understanding of the technology solutions. One of my clients, for example, reported great success from merely stopping by his key client's office weekly. He said his client's perception was that customer service had improved over the last few months. It's amazing what a little personal attention can do. In today's environment, our clients are often geographically dispersed, requiring more creativity to stay in touch. Technology does enable us to communicate, but resorting back to voice communications may provide even more relational contact. For example, one IT leader I've worked with schedules regular coffee breaks on the phone, essentially 15-minute check-ins to see how things are going with her clients. Remember, if you're not influencing your client, someone else is.

4. The opportunity to have the greatest influence is to step fully into the *Problem-Solving Partner* role. The analogy that I use for this role is that you and your client are getting into the same car to navigate a road trip. You decide together where you're going and how you're going to get there. You both bring valuable perspectives that need to be

considered along the way. When you encounter an unexpected problem, there's no blaming. You reassess your options and proceed. When the journey is over, you celebrate your accomplishments and share the lessons learned for the next trip.

This last role is one that appears to take more time. But my experience has shown that the upfront time involved pays you in dividends at the back end because you get the job done right the first time. For projects that are complex and involve a host of sponsors, you can't afford not to have everyone in the car when you begin the journey.

The technical wizard and technical assistant are often the roles in which the IT department builds a solid reputation. When your business clients have confidence in your ability to deliver value, they will be receptive to your role as silent influencer or problem-solving partner.

So, How Do I Become a Consultant?

For most IT organizations, transitioning into the role of consultant requires a fundamental shift in approach and mindset, as well as the development of a new set of skills. Historically, technology expertise may have gotten you hired, but today, it's business acumen that gets you invited to the table, and it's human interaction capabilities that will get you invited back.

Today, I find more and more examples of individuals being hired because of their business savvy, and they're taught the technology skills needed. Clients will have confidence in you if you know where to go to obtain in-depth technology knowledge, as long as you fully understand the business realities.

In some cases, IT even hires for personal interaction skills. I know of one CIO who five years ago stopped hiring programmers to get the technology skills he needed on staff. Instead, he began hiring people who were strong in interpersonal skills and then sent them to the local community college to gain technology skills. His goal was to create a team that could create a strong connection with the business. And hands-down, he tells me, these are the programmers that the rest of the organization consistently requests to be on their project teams.

At the same time, it's important for IT leaders to create a spreadsheet of its technology competencies and weaknesses. There needs to be a plan to be sure resources are there to meet future needs, whether in the form of outside experts or bulking up training efforts. It's simply impossible for everyone on the team to stay current with one's skills, with technology changing at today's current pace. Today's IT leader is responsible for determining the best mix of resources, both internal and external.

Let's take a closer look at the business and communication skills that IT leaders and their staffs need to develop to become more consultative. It starts with IT professionals taking full responsibility for the messages they communicate and the impact it has on others.

Business Acumen

When it comes to developing business acumen, the goal is to educate yourself and your staff on the clients' areas of expertise and the current business pressures they face. How do you do this? Mainly by spending time with clients, watching how they interact with existing technology in their day-to-day work life, and asking good questions when you're approached for a technology change or new system. You and your staff need to become students of the business and learn enough to speak the client's language and understand their real issues.

This requires developing good interview skills. For example, before launching into a new project, IT professionals should ask clients what issues they're trying to resolve, what they're trying to accomplish, and why that's such a concern for the business. During this conversation, you need to work to identify the root problem the client is having—you may find the client doesn't need a new system at all but a feature that's already available in an existing application or that could be built through a simple modification. We cover interview skills in more depth in Chapter 7, on gathering business requirements.

Or it could be the opposite—the client may think it's a simple request to just add another column to a spreadsheet, without understanding that this request involves accessing data from another database. In the end, it might be better to solve the issue manually and use IT resources for something with higher payback.

It's only by understanding the business environment as well as the challenges, responsibilities, and pressures that clients face that IT can apply technology in the most effective way possible.

Human Interaction Skills

Perhaps even more important, most IT professionals also need to strengthen their communication skills in order to interact with clients effectively. While left-brained skills such as analytical thinking, logical reasoning, and sequential capabilities are important for the systems-building side of the job, consulting requires right-brained skills such as listening, empathy, and dealing with emotions.

Here are some of the more important human interaction skills IT leaders and their staffs need to develop.

AUDIENCE PROFILE Few IT departments have the luxury of starting from scratch in building a relationship with their clients.

There's usually some history, either positive or negative. One important skill is learning to develop an audience profile. Who exactly is your client? Identify what you know, what will affect the project, the client's technical savvy, and the past history with IT. Do your business clients trust the IT department and have confidence in its capabilities, or is there some repair work that needs to be done?

Clearly, you'd use a different strategy to influence a client who's on board and enthusiastic about getting a new initiative started versus one who feels she has been burned in previous systems projects. You can't just leave that elephant standing in the room. But remember, once you start talking about the elephant, it's important to hear out the client's grievances without becoming defensive, even if you think they're completely wrong. It's important to acknowledge any issues in your organization's history with the client and lay out a plan to regain his trust.

LISTENING   You might think of listening as a passive activity. But good listening actually requires a lot of work if you want to ensure that you understand what you hear, absorb it, and act on it with any degree of accuracy.

Active listeners aren't silent during the exchange; rather they clarify what they hear, paraphrase what they think they understand, and ensure that they're not making incorrect assumptions. We all filter what we hear, either adding extra details or skipping over points that we deem unimportant but that may be crucial.

Indeed, incorrect assumptions are the bane of any listener. Even seemingly simple words can mean vastly different things to different people. What would you think if a client says he needs to see a system in 20 days—that he wants to be up and running with reporting capabilities in that short time frame? Or that he wants to see a plan or a high-level design? It's not unlike the classic cartoon portraying a client asking for a swing, and different developers picture everything from a tire swing to an executive chair hanging from a tree. You need to clarify, paraphrase, and play back the speaker's words to ensure you have an accurate understanding.

I like to illustrate this in my workshops with the following exercise: I ask one person to relay an event that takes around 60 seconds to tell. Then I ask someone who was listening to retell the story as accurately as she can. The reteller is almost always surprised by the extra details she adds and the pieces she leaves out because of the assumptions she made while listening.

EMPATHY It's easier to work through any type of grievance when you develop the ability to respond empathetically. After all, demonstrating empathy doesn't mean you're agreeing with the client's point of view but that you're willing to acknowledge and respect it. It's the difference between saying, "I completely agree with everything you're saying" and "I completely understand everything you're saying." And it starts by vocalizing your desire to understand the other person's point of view. For example, "I can see you're frustrated—help me understand what's going on so I can see things better from your perspective."

The more empathetic you are, the more you demonstrate to the client that you understand his reality. That gives him the confidence that you'll be able to work through future issues constructively.

For many in IT, I find this to be an Achilles heel. Far too often, the IT professional's gut instinct is to defend herself, cut off the other person, or flat out make her wrong. "After all," they figure, "We've done our homework and know the right answer." But being an effective consultant isn't about *the right answer*. If others can't hear what you have to say because of how you deliver the message, you have lost your ability to influence. Delivery is everything. If I have an important point to make, the other person is much more likely to hear me if I have been equally interested in his perspective. How I demonstrate that respect is empathy. In most conversations, that can be a simple paraphrase or acknowledgment of his idea first, before I add my two cents.

DIPLOMACY   Closely related to empathy is diplomacy, which is being respectful to other people even when you don't agree with them. After all, you're not going to influence anyone with the attitude of, "I'm right, and you're an idiot." Or even, "You're wrong, and here's why."

When you find yourself disagreeing with a client—even when you're sure you're right—you have to keep it from becoming a battle of who's right and who's wrong. You need to take a step back and deliver your message in a way that the other person wants to listen to it.

Sometimes, it's even a matter of helping the other person save face—it's embarrassing and threatening for someone to realize she's wrong. So, it's important to create a safe environment for the other person to become more knowledgeable and perhaps even change her opinion.

AVOIDING EMOTIONAL HOOKS   It's easy to get upset or angry when the people you're dealing with go on the attack or annoy you in other ways, like refusing to validate your competence or insisting their viewpoint is right. For many people, their first reaction is to push back, defend themselves, or throw up their hands and walk away. It's the fight-or-flight instinct. But once you're emotionally hooked, you are no longer objective, and your effectiveness as a consultant is diminished.

That's why another important skill to adopt for yourself and to teach your staff is developing the awareness to know what stirs your most passionate emotional responses. With this self-awareness, you can avoid taking other people's words personally, stay objective, and see the situation for what it is.

At one client I've worked with, I was very intrigued by a development strategy one of the IT directors used with her staff. This is a world-renowned medical institution that really does deal with life-or-death issues. This director saw the value in helping her staff handle those sticky situations better. She knew that when tough situations are handled poorly, it can cause damage to key relationships. This director regularly stages fire drills at staff meetings based on real situations encountered in the past, to let the team practice managing their way through difficult emotional encounters. How would they react when a business unit vice president dresses them down and tells them they're a bunch of idiots who don't know what they're doing? By practicing their response, they'll have better options and more confidence when a similar event occurs in real life.

EDUCATING WITHOUT ARROGANCE   I've heard many IT departments complain that clients don't really know what they want, that they're unable to provide a clear set of requirements. But that would be akin to asking the client to provide a blueprint of a house when they've never built one before. It's up to the IT professional to educate business clients on what they don't know and do it in a way the client can understand. This is also a problem for those in IT who have other IT functional areas as clients. Even within IT, we don't always speak the same language. The same words can have very different meanings. In fact, I have found this to be an even bigger challenge with IT clients because we make many more assumptions when we think we understand.

First, you have to educate yourself on the language the client speaks and how to translate your knowledge in a way that works for the client. And remember that just because IT professionals tend to be analytical and linear in their thinking, not everyone else is. And just because IT professionals tend to lay out the facts in a logical way, that doesn't mean the client will understand. You need to turn the tables around—what matters to them? What are their goals? What misperceptions do they have?

You also have to learn how to share your knowledge and expertise without being threatening, negative, arrogant, or condescending. This often means being conscious of your word choices and tone of voice. Your goal is to help the client feel more confident, secure, and engaged in the project.

For example, what if the client is asking for changes that are outside the available time and budget constraints? The client assumes IT can work its magic and produce a system that does what he needs. The temptation might be to tell him how unrealistic his request is. But what if you helped him become a better consumer of technology by educating him on what his request entails? Then, you could dig in to what he's really asking for and agree to something that's close to what he wants—something that's "good enough."

When you do this, you're also helping to market your organization, something that's discussed in Chapter 9. Negative stereotypes aside, marketing is simply creating an awareness of your value by educating and communicating with clients.

RAPPORT BUILDING Because of the time constraints facing IT departments today, many IT professionals consider it a goal to stick to the facts and minimize socializing during meetings and encounters with business clients. But what if they developed a closer relationship with the client? What kind of benefits would that provide?

Consider this scenario: You arrive in a client's cubicle for a scheduled one-on-one meeting, and she's excited about an e-mail she just received with photographs from the previous weekend's celebration of her grandmother's ninetieth birthday. She invites you to have a look before you start the meeting. How would you respond?

All too often, IT professionals might say, "We've got a lot to do today—can we continue with our agenda?" What a missed opportunity! This was the perfect chance to share a personal moment with the client and thus build some rapport.

I always recommend that you take your cues from the client. The bottom line is that people are much more willing to give others the benefit of the doubt if they feel a mutual connection. These encounters don't have to get touch-feely, but, for example, if you see pictures of the client's child playing soccer on the desk, why not ask a few questions about it? It will only help you in the future, especially when a project gets rocky. With some individuals, you'll need to build rapport totally around the business because you may know very little about them personally.

Building rapport with individuals who are geographically dispersed requires more intentionality. I know many teams that send digital pictures to introduce themselves, and they make sure that if someone on the team is traveling to that location, to schedule a time to stop in and make personal contact. When working with global clients, rapport building often requires even more social contact and establishment of personal relationships.

How Difficult Can This Be?

Like anything in life, the idea of developing consulting skills and learning to influence other people is simpler than the reality of doing so. For one thing, it requires IT and business clients to learn about each other's areas of expertise, and it takes time to do that. Amid the pressure today to just do it, you may face some pushback. But in the end, it's more time consuming to *not* approach things this way.

One business analyst I know was struck by an experience he had outside of work that really drove home this point. He and his wife wanted to add a fireplace to their home. They called three contractors, one of whom never called back and one who gave his bid over the phone. The third, however, asked if he could come to the analyst's house to meet him and his wife and see the room in which they wanted the fireplace. He drew up some sketches of different approaches, showing them what was possible, what it would involve, and the cost for each idea. In the end, his bid was higher than the phone bid, but the analyst and his wife were hooked—they felt this contractor really understood what they wanted, and they looked forward to working with him, as they had really developed a good rapport.

Did this take extra time? Sure it did, but the analyst and his wife were nearly guaranteed to be satisfied with the final outcome. Balancing the pressure to just do it and taking time to more clearly understand a client's needs will result in greater value. If you're not convinced, think of how your outside competition responds to your clients' requests for an IT solution—"Sure, we can do that!"—without really understanding the details.

Another reason you may get pushback is because of the IT organization's previous history with the client. Does the client have reason to trust that the organization would be a good partner, ready and able to operate as a valued consultant? If past experience has shown clients that working with IT takes too much time, money, and effort, there's some reputation rebuilding to do.

This applies even if you just joined the company, and the bad experience with IT took place five years before. Clients can draw the conclusion after one debacle. They often paint all IT departments with the same brush. For better or worse, IT walks around with whatever baggage was created by previous experience, good, bad, or indifferent.

At one client I worked with, a business executive recounted to me when the CIO at the firm had announced a new organizational structure to better align the department with the business. "We laughed," the executive says. "We had not historically heard IT talk about the business at all—it was always about technology. So when they declared they wanted to be strategic business partners, we couldn't imagine it."

It took the CIO two years to establish the credibility the IT department needed to start partnering with the business. It involved building best practices, demonstrating an interest in understanding the business, and talking with clients in their language.

It's not easy starting from behind the eight ball, but when you consider all the options, what better choice could you make? Our clients need a trusted partner to enable the business strategies that they're putting in place right now. Don't you want to be perceived as their partner of choice?

Conclusion

Business clients make decisions every day, big and small, and for those that involve technology, they need to work with someone they trust, a partner who can help them sort out what they really need from what they think they want. Like a good Realtor, contractor, financial planner, or doctor, IT professionals need to become that kind of partner—someone with both the technology expertise and the ability to apply it in ways that make them indispensable to the business.

And indispensable is exactly what IT organizations need to be. You need to put aside any preconceived notions of what a consultant does and realize that you need to become an internal consultant, yourself. Otherwise, there are plenty of external vendors and consultants who will happily do that job for you. But just like them, you can develop the skills and mindsets to influence your clients and—by doing so—they'll give you the opportunity to help make decisions that are best for both the business and the IT organization.

There's really no other choice for IT professionals today. You can either be the broker who lets her clients make the wrong investments for their needs—never to be called upon by those clients again—or you can develop the business acumen and human interaction skills that are the marks of a trusted partner.

Top Ten

Considerations for Evolving into the Role of Consultant

10. Stop making assumptions—paraphrase to check your understanding. Own the communications.

9. If you call a meeting, make it a good one.

8. If you're not bringing enthusiasm to work, you may be draining it from others (if you don't like what you're doing, it shows).

7. Ask good questions—uncover the issue instead of rushing in with a fix.

6. Learn diplomacy—be respectful even when you don't agree.

5. Deliver your message in way that others can hear it—avoid appearing arrogant and condescending.

4. Talk about what you can do, not what you can't—clients don't want to hear excuses; they want help solving their problem.

3. If trust breaks down, you need to address it head-on—ask your client what it will take to rebuild the relationship.

(continued)

(*continued*)

2. Educate clients to be better consumers of technology—you can play a huge role in increasing their confidence in your services.

1. When you take the position of being right, it implies someone else is wrong—or worse, an idiot. Instead, take time to listen so you can understand the other's perspective first.

Specific Actions I Will Take

-
-
-

CHAPTER 5

Negotiating: Getting What You Want without Damaging the Relationship

Not a day goes by that IT leaders and staff members don't negotiate with someone. My definition for *negotiations* is that it is what happens when someone wants something from someone else, whether that person is a team member or a business client. Typically, each party states its case, and in one way or another, they come to an agreement, whether they're skilled or unskilled, and whether the process is emotional or not.

Think of a day in the life of the IT organization, in which IT professionals at all levels of the organization face many types of negotiation situations every day, all day long. Before launching a new application, they need to work with the business client to have them allocate some of their staff to test the application. Then they need to work with the IT server team to get the go-ahead to get some space on a server for testing. From there, they need to secure a slot on the applications staff's calendar to make sure the test system is loaded in time for the business group they just talked into doing the testing. Their success at securing these needed resources hinges on their ability to negotiate with clients and other IT staff.

Think about the help desk and various technical support staff, who need negotiation skills to ensure that clients with critical needs don't get stuck in a queue waiting for IT support. And hardware techs often need to negotiate with software techs when coordinating upgrades for clients who simply can't wait six weeks for new application or technology capabilities. Clearly, the need for negotiation skills is as important to IT leaders as it is to their staffs. Money, people, and time are all scarce in today's business world, and IT professionals are called upon to negotiate constantly for them.

However, the IT professionals I deal with usually lack the confidence for the negotiations that happen every day in the IT environment. Many like to believe that negotiating is what gets done on the vendor management team, and that it has nothing to do with leaders and staff personnel. And even if they are aware of how much they need to negotiate, many IT professionals are not at all sure how to do it and tend to avoid it. In fact, during my 27 years as a consultant and workshop leader at O&A, I've talked to IT professionals who are constantly understaffed, don't have the right resources, and need to meet unrealistic deadlines, all because of poor negotiation skills.

It doesn't have to be that way. It's my belief that to succeed in the IT profession today, all of IT—including IT leaders and the people who report to them—must get past their aversion to negotiating and learn how to manage the conflict that's an inevitable part of their everyday lives.

The good news is, good negotiators aren't born; they're taught. In fact, for a long time, I've strongly believed that IT could do a better job negotiating if they learned about something called *interest negotiations* rather than using *position negotiations,* both of which I talk about later in this chapter. And on a personal note, while I was in the process of developing the negotiation workshop for O&A, my belief was strengthened even further when I went through the process of selling my home. My own negotiations cemented for me the difference between interest negotiations and position negotiations,

78

and as a result, I was able to get more out of the deal than I ever thought possible.

The most important thing about learning to be a skilled negotiator is changing your mindset about conflict and understanding that it's not something to avoid or downplay—it's a necessary component of two parties working out a difference of opinion. Conflict is an essential and inevitable part of life, so it's crucial to accept it and become aware of your own individual way of handling it. It is neither good nor bad; it's just a difference of opinion.

In the rest of this chapter, I provide an overview of other key mindset changes, as well as the negotiating skills and tools that I've learned about and found to be most effective in the IT world. Some of these concepts are informed by the highly influential negotiating reference books *Getting to Yes,* by Roger Fisher, and William Ury[1] and *Bargaining for Advantage* by G. Richard Shell.[2]

Position versus *Interest* Negotiations

Picture this scenario: Let's say your staff is working with the sales department on a project to set up a client-tracking system for the sales force. Your staff says it needs four people, two months, and $25,000 to complete the project, while the sales department says it's willing to pay for two people, needs the system in three weeks, and can budget only $10,000.

Can you feel the tension building? Does it seem inevitable that this conflict will quickly devolve into what some call *position negotiation,* in which both IT and the client plant their stakes ever more firmly into the ground, each wondering why the heck the other can't understand their point of view? Certainly this is no way to start or maintain a good relationship with a client, let alone begin a project.

It doesn't have to be that way. In general, the customary practice in the United States is to try to resolve differences by negotiating based on *position* rather than on *interest*. But it's not the only approach.

Look at a hypothetical scenario. Imagine two students, Jason and Sam, sitting across from one another at a table in a dorm room studying. Directly to their left is a window. Jason's position is that he wants the window closed, and Sam's position is that he wants it open. They begin negotiating by each taking a *position*. By taking positions, they find themselves at extremes—an open versus closed window. The physical position of the window is the only item they are negotiating about because of the stakes they've put in the ground.

This negotiating style is inefficient and often ineffective. Positions limit negotiations because there's not a lot to negotiate over, and they create linear situations, with the participants starting at extreme endpoints and then moving along the continuum to some point at which both agree to agree. In the case of Jason and Sam, the continuum is the physical window position—they can agree to have it completely open, completely closed, or at some point in between. It will take a lot of time to come to an agreement because they started at extreme endpoints and will only make small concessions, which take time and energy. This also endangers the relationship because it becomes a contest of wills, and anger and resentment often results.

The alternative negotiating method is to negotiate based on our interests. Look at Jason's interests for wanting the window closed: There's a draft directly on his shoulder, and he's just getting over a cold and doesn't want to get sick again. He's only wearing a light short-sleeved shirt. The noise outside the window is distracting his studying.

Meanwhile, Sam might be pulling an all-nighter and wants the cool air to help keep him awake. He doesn't have a cell phone and is waiting for his friend to yell up to him from the parking lot below to let him know he's arrived.

By talking about interests, the scope of potential negotiating possibilities increases dramatically. The two of them now can generate a list of options based on the different interests they have just stated. Jason might negotiate about changing seats with Sam so the draft isn't on his shoulders. Sam might get some coffee to keep him awake. Jason might suggest that Sam have his friend call him on Jason's cell phone when he arrives. They might agree to open a totally different window that would give Sam some air but not directly affect Jason. They are now discussing multiple options that have nothing to do with the physical position of the window—in fact, the window doesn't even come up in the discussion, whereas it was the only thing they were discussing before.

That's because interests define each party's real needs, wants, or concerns. They are broader than and can be very different from stated positions. When you understand your own interests as well as those of the other party, you can spend your time developing possible options, not fighting over small concessions about one item.

Let's go back to the sales example introduced earlier. The typical negotiating method would be for the IT department to start from its end of the three positions (number of people, time, and budget), while the sales department starts from the other end of the same three positions. The two sides would move linearly toward each other, hopefully coming to a common ground both can agree on. This is *position* negotiating. The options are limited, which makes the negotiation results very limited.

But what if the IT department's *interests* include the fact that the department is about to hire two new people who will start in three weeks. This small sales project would be a perfect way of getting the new hires familiar with their new environment, rather than starting them immediately on a complex project. The sales department has two people leaving for extended leave and wants them trained before they go, so that when they return, the ramp-up time is quicker.

Now IT and sales can broaden their negotiating stand. IT might stick with its time frame of two months but offer to do the project with five people instead of four, while lowering the budget from $25,000 to $10,000. IT might even suggest to sales that if it expands the budget to $25,000 and is willing to wait two months, it will add a whole bunch of desirable bells and whistles to the program. At this point, IT has moved away from the linearity of position negotiating (two versus four people, three weeks versus two months, $10,000 versus $25,000) to something much broader, such as training new hires (which is an interest of IT) and expanding the scope of the project (which is an interest of sales). They can also offer to train the sales force on a prototype before they leave, therefore helping speed up their use of the new system later.

Three Key Factors; Three-Step Process

When we think about negotiating, we often picture two parties sitting across from each other at the bargaining table. But in actuality, there are three steps to the negotiating process: planning and preparation, the information exchange, and, finally, bargaining. And in each of these steps, we need to address three key factors: negotiating elements; people and relationships; and styles and situations.

I like to depict the three-step process as a stairway, and the three key factors as a railing (see Figure 5.1). The railing supports each step of the stairway, and you have to ascend the stairway one step at a time, without skipping any step.

In my workshops, I start by discussing the railing—or the three key factors—as we look at the first step: preparation and planning. Anyone who's ever painted a room in his house has discovered—either the easy way or the hard way—that planning and preparation are as important as and can take longer than the

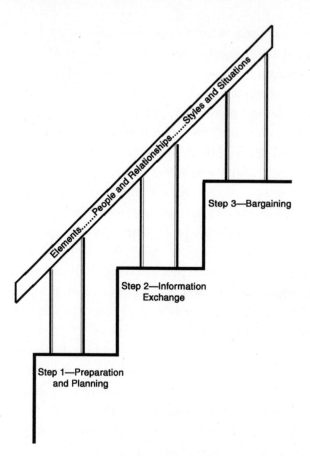

FIGURE 5.1 Three-Step Negotiation Process

actual painting. The same can be said of negotiating, and yet many people involved with negotiations fail to expend the effort on this stage that they should.

Standing on this first step, we begin to establish the first key factor on the railing—our negotiation elements.

Negotiation Elements

The first element involves assessing your positions, interests, and options, as well as those of the other party. This means analyzing what's important to you and your clients in regard to positions, interests, and options. So whereas your position is something you've decided on ("we can finish that project in three months"), your interests are what caused you to make that decision ("we've got five other projects going on," "we just lost a key database analyst," and so on). Everyone in virtually every situation has multiple interests, and these need to be brought to the table so that you aren't limited by positions.

That's why you want to list *all* of your interests before you sit down at the negotiating table. The typical items IT negotiates about are money, time (due date), people (resources), scope, standards, policies, and procedures. If you understand your own interests, you're in a much better position to be creative about the options you propose and how you respond to those that are proposed to you.

Let's take another look at Jason and Sam. If Sam understood his need to stay awake as an interest, he could have concentrated on other options that would keep him awake besides the physical position of the window. You're in a much better position if you can stay flexible, and that means being prepared to offer and accept a range of options.

But it's not a one-way street—it's also important to understand the needs and concerns of your clients so you can anticipate what their reactions are likely to be and what leverage they might have over you. Do some background work to determine the other party's interests and options.

You also need to establish some criteria that you and the other party can use as a fair measurement of whether you've reached an equitable agreement. For example, are there some industry best practices you can use to establish the amount of time you need to complete the project? Or maybe, if you've had a successful project with this client in the past, you can suggest using the same benchmarks as the criteria for starting negotiations on this project. For example, if you dedicated two days a week to the past project and it was successful, you can suggest doing the same on this project.

You also need to think about leverage. Leverage is created from the balance of fears and needs, based on which side has more to lose from a failure to agree. So, the more a party has to lose, the less leverage it has, and the less it has to lose, the more leverage it has.

Two additional pieces of information that need to be considered are your bottom line and your BATNA (best alternative to a negotiated agreement). Your bottom line defines what you absolutely can't yield on. Meanwhile, BATNA is a concept developed by negotiation researchers Roger Fisher, William Ury, and Bruce Patton. It refers to the courses of action that are at your disposal if the current negotiations fail—in other words, your Plan B.

Knowing your BATNA helps you know when to walk away from the negotiations. For example, if you know you can resell something—say a car—to a used dealer for $10,000, the bottom line helps you be better equipped to resist making a bad decision, such as selling it for $7,000 in the pressure of the moment. To determine your BATNA, you would also take into consideration the steps you would have to take if the negotiations were to fail. For example, you would have to find a buyer other than the used car dealer, and you'd have to pay to advertise the car, research the required paperwork, and possibly even postpone your new car purchase. Knowing what your alternative steps are if you walk away from the negotiations helps you be more flexible than just having a bottom line because you can readily compare your alternative plan to what's on the table. It may sometimes be worth putting aside your set bottom line because the alterative options if you walk away are not as good as what is currently on the table. When you reach the point that your alternatives (BATNA) are better than what you are being offered in the negotiations, this tells you to walk away.

People and Relationships

Further along the railing but still on the first step, we address the second key factor: people and relationships. During this phase, you need to assess the degree of trust you have with the people you're negotiating with and work to repair any poor or non-existent relationships.

It's easy to overlook the importance of relationships during negotiations and focus only on substance. In my work with IT clients, I find most are more comfortable discussing things versus feelings. But avoiding relationship issues is only an option if you have no intention of ever dealing with the people you're negotiating with again. Most often, that's not the case for IT professionals, who deal mainly with internal clients. Once a project ends, you're bound to work with these same people again, down the road.

For this reason, it's really important not to blow the relationship, and ideally, you should strive to strengthen the relationship so that the next project gets off to an even better start. When a relationship is good, it creates trust and confidence, which can help smooth over the rough spots in future negotiations. Without it, even relatively easy negotiations can be difficult. The relationship-building process is more fully discussed in Chapter 4, on consulting skills.

Styles and Situations

The last key factor on the railing is styles and situations. During the planning and preparation step, you need to determine your own negotiating style, as well as that of the other party. Most people actually have two or three preferred styles, based on the way they prefer to handle conflict. Using *Bargaining for*

Advantage and the Thomas-Kilmann Conflict Mode Instrument, I define five different styles, ranging from passive to aggressive:

1. *Competitors:* Like to win and control negotiations by using demands, threats, and ultimatums.
2. *Problem solvers:* Encourage each party to talk about their interests and then find a solution by brainstorming many options. This style works well in complex negotiations, but it's not so practical when time is short or the other party isn't willing to work with you.
3. *Compromisers:* Look for quick, obvious, and fair solutions to bargaining problems, like splitting the difference.
4. *Accommodators:* Tend to resolve interpersonal conflicts by solving the other person's problem.
5. *Avoiders:* Strongly dislike interpersonal conflict and try to avoid situations that might cause conflict. They try very hard to arrange their personal and professional lives so that conflict is at a minimum.[3]

You also have to take your best guess at the style of the person you're negotiating with. Don't assume the other party approaches conflict the same way you do, or you could get your lunch eaten. Imagine an accommodator assuming that a competitor also wants to help solve the opposing party's problems!

In addition to assessing your client's negotiation style, you also have to think about the bargaining situation you're entering into. There are four basic situations, and each one is based on two characteristics: the importance of the substance you're negotiating on and the importance of the future relationship you have with the opposing party.

Figure 5.2—based on *Bargaining for Advantage*—illustrates the four situations. In the top two quadrants, the importance of the future relationship with the opposing party is high. These are the most common bargaining situations for IT professionals,

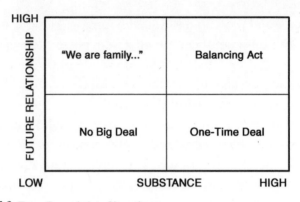

FIGURE 5.2 Four Bargaining Situations

who almost always negotiate with people they'll need to work with again in the future.

In the top left quadrant, the substance of the negotiations is less important than the relationship you're trying to build, maintain, or mend. For example, you might be willing to throw in more bells and whistles or charge less if you're just getting to know a new client or are trying to repair a poor relationship. The emphasis is on the relationship, not the substance being negotiated.

The upper right quadrant represents the situation I feel IT professionals find themselves in most of the time. The relationship is very important, but with limited budgets and resources, you can't just give away the farm, so the substance of the conflict is also important. That's why I call it the "balancing act." In this situation, you have to be prepared to not back down in negotiations and make promises on substance issues that you can't keep (that is, dates, scope, priorities). Otherwise, despite your best efforts, the client will see only missed deadlines and failed delivery. At the same time, focusing only on substance and ignoring the relationship can destroy the project just as quickly.

The bottom two quadrants happen less often. The lower left quadrant is a situation in which the relationship and the substance of negotiations are equally low in importance. It might be a quick favor for one person who needs to accomplish something that's not particularly strategic to the company, like a simple report. It's not a big deal, it takes little time, and it has no impact on future dealings.

A one-time deal, on the other hand, is when the substance is more important than the relationship. It's easy to make the mistake of thinking you're in this type of bargaining situation when you're really not. For example, a client may ask you to install a new release or code some extra features. You see this as just more work (that is, as a substance issue). Many IT professionals will want to negotiate only on substance and tell the client, "No, it's outside of scope." That's when it's time to do some homework to assess how important the request is to the client's business and whether you can take the opportunity to strengthen the relationship with this client by doing something about the substantive issue.

Applying the Key Factors to the Second Step: Information Exchange

Now we move up to step two, the information exchange. In this phase, you meet face to face with the opposing party, but you're not in the bargaining phase yet. Whereas the first step was all about doing lots of preliminary legwork and researching the three key factors, the second step is when you can really see if your assessments are correct, and can clear up and get information you don't have. It's time for both parties to get their perceptions out in the open, and state their interests and issues.

Through conversation and observation, you determine during the information exchange things such as whether you were right about the client's interests and opinions, whether they trust IT as much as you thought they did, whether you guessed correctly at their bargaining style, and if you're in the bargaining situation you thought you were in. It's when you can really see whether you were right about your assessments during the planning and preparation step.

For example, I might sit down with the client, thinking I'm coming into a "balancing act" situation (upper right quadrant), in which both the substance of the negotiations and the relationship have equal importance. But I'm unaware that before I joined the company, they'd worked on a major project with IT that ended in disaster. During the information exchange, I ask them if this is their first major project with the IT organization, and they answer with an emotional description of the former debacle.

Finding this out, I need to correct my assessment and readjust for a "We are family" bargaining situation (upper left quadrant), since I've determined the relationship is shaky and needs to be strengthened.

Here's another example: I had never met the particular client before, but I researched what he was like by talking with others who had worked with him. Through that legwork, I determined that he typically uses a compromiser style in negotiations. During the information exchange, I look around his office and ask him about his golf trophies. He responds by telling me he loves golf but hates team sports because he doesn't like to depend on other people to help him win. With that comment, I realize he's more of a competitor than a compromiser and plan to adjust my bargaining style accordingly.

Notice that this second step is all about dialogue, relationship building, and establishing rapport. Put simply, no one is going to tell you anything until she trusts you. If you want to hear the other person's interests and point of view, you need to build a rapport. So if you have a poor relationship with the client, make sure you mend it before moving to the bargaining step. Building rapport and relationships is discussed in more detail in Chapter 4 on consulting skills.

It's also important during this second step to actively listen to what the client has to say. Active listening means you ask questions when you don't understand what is being said and paraphrase your understanding of what the client is saying. This isn't the time to argue or shut down the dialogue. The most important thing during the information exchange stage is to keep the dialogue flowing, even if you find yourself vehemently disagreeing with the other party. Once the dialogue ends, the negotiations are over. In my workshops, I teach a method called "disagreeing diplomatically," which focuses on keeping a discussion going when you want to say no.

The Final Step: Now Comes the Bargaining

Finally, we move to the top and final step: bargaining. In this step, you use all the information you've gathered and vetted in the first and second steps. You know your own interests and options as well as the opposing party's. You've established criteria and your bottom line. You're sure of the bargaining situation you're getting into, the negotiation style you're going to use, and the style you're going to encounter. Now you're ready to bargain.

Bargaining is mainly made up of exchanges, concessions, and dealmaking. It's where you determine who will give and get what. It's also where you will likely encounter tactics that are used differently by people depending on their different negotiating styles.

What's important to realize is that people with different negotiation styles have different views of what's fair and ethical. The tactics you decide to use are very much intertwined in the kind of person you are—you can't separate the way you act in negotiations from the person you are in life. The best advice is to let your conscience be your guide.

Meanwhile, it's very important to recognize when tactics are being used negatively against you and what your possible counter moves should be. Knowing how to respond beforehand will keep you from reacting emotionally. Here are five of the most common bargaining tactics I've seen people use over my years in the IT profession:

1. *The hot potato:* They get you to take on their problem by making it your problem. A good countermove is to refuse to take ownership and instead generate options they can take.

2. *Appeal to a higher authority:* They postpone a decision to take it to someone of greater authority. A good countermove is to find out what they *are* able to commit to before you begin bargaining.

3. *The flinch:* They try to get concessions by having you react to their overstated emotion, usually a dramatic verbal or nonverbal negative response to a proposal. A good countermove is to not react emotionally and show confusion as a reaction to their outburst.

4. *Nibbling:* The goal of this is to try to get a little bit more out of you once the other party thinks the negotiations are over. The extra issue or demand is so small, it doesn't sound worth spoiling the deal after so much investment. A good countermove is to offer to open up negotiations all over again to include this new item.

5. *Reciprocity ploys:* They make small concessions while asking you for big ones. A good countermove is to take a break when you feel pressured and consider the overall situation before making your next move.

Conclusion: Effective Negotiators Are Made, Not Born

Many IT professionals might feel new to the negotiations scene, or they might think negotiations don't include them, but that's not true. Negotiations are something people in IT engage in every day, with peers, subordinates, bosses, and clients. And the only way to feel more comfortable and confident in this role is to learn about the techniques that experienced negotiators employ and practice them consistently.

A good place to begin is to realize that negotiating doesn't start at the bargaining table. It takes time to plan and prepare your side—both your position and your interests—and find out the same about your client. The more options and interests you bring to the table and the more flexibility you have, the better deal you can make.

I hear IT professionals claim they just don't have the time to engage in this three-step process. What they need to realize is that it's more than time spent; it's an investment made—an investment that will serve them in developing and maintaining better relationships, more reasonable deadlines, adequate resources, and positive outcomes. Resources are scarce in today's business world, and we're called upon to negotiate constantly for them, in the form of money, people, and time. If you want the resources you need, and the relationships that help you get them, you've got to become a skilled negotiator and teach your staff to do the same.

Remember that no one is asking you to be something you're not. There are all sorts of negotiating styles; it's up to you to determine which one is right for you. At the end of the day, you still need to have a relationship with the other party after the negotiations end. It's a fine balance between getting what you and the other party needs and maintaining a healthy business relationship with our clients.

Getting your head in the negotiating game doesn't have to be stressful. It's all about confronting your anxieties, changing your mindset, being yourself, and—perhaps most important of all—knowing how to prepare.

Top Ten

Approaches for Getting What You Want without Damaging the Relationship

10. Remember Ben Franklin's words: "If you fail to prepare, you prepare to fail."
9. The single-answer approach inhibits creating options. Be flexible and open to various options.
8. Relationships and rapport count.
7. Know your preferred negotiation styles.
6. Be clear on which of the four bargaining situations you are negotiating within.
5. The cheapest concession to give the other party is to listen to them.
4. Don't close the negotiation door by saying "no"; disagree diplomatically.
3. Be prepared to recognize tactics during bargaining and to counter them effectively.
2. Be aware that you negotiate every day, within your IT team and with clients, and learn from each experience.
1. The benefits of effective negotiations: You improve the chances you will get what you need and want, and you'll keep your client relationship solid.

Specific Actions I Will Take

-
-
-

Notes

[1] Roger Fisher and William Ury, *Getting to Yes: Negotiating Agreements without Giving In* (New York: Penguin, 1991).

[2]G. Richard Shell, *Bargaining for Advantage: Negotiation Strategies for Reasonable People* (New York: Penguin Group, 2006).

[3]———, *Bargaining for Advantage: Negotiation Strategies for Reasonable People* (New York: Penguin Group, 2006); Kenneth Thomas and Ralph Kilmann, *Thomas-Kilmann Conflict Mode Instrument* (Santa Clara, CA: Xicom, 1974).

CHAPTER 6

Managing Projects: The Science and the Art

It's a generally agreed-upon statistic that about 25 percent of technology projects are deemed successful. If the engineering field had the same number of project failures, no one would ever ride in an elevator or fly in an airplane! Whether you concur with this abysmal statistic or not, I think we can all agree that it's time we boost our project success rate.

The fact is, IT project management is a relatively young discipline, especially when compared with other industries. In construction, engineering, and defense contracting, project management is significantly better understood, supported, and practiced, and project managers and their clients in these fields generally benefit from a higher level of professional maturity. They can rely on documented historical records of prior project undertakings, more formal authority granted to the project manager, enhanced regulatory and QA oversight, greater emphasis on formal educational qualifications, mandatory licensing and certification requirements, genuine legal liability for malfeasance or poor quality, and a more responsible understanding of the role of project sponsor. Does any of this sound even vaguely familiar within the world of IT?

In 1981, the Project Management Institute (PMI) set out a goal to establish project management as a unique discipline and an independent profession. It has been incredibly successful in meeting that goal. Project management is the predominant management style of the twenty-first century, complete with professional certification and a growing body of knowledge.

Yet for all the acknowledgment of the importance of project management to modern companies, the role of the IT project manager is often tenuous at best. During my 20 years as an independent consultant, I have witnessed too many instances of what can be described only as project management malpractice. Even the selection and development of project managers is so often dictated by convenience or corporate inertia that it can be regarded as the accidental profession.

On one hand, IT projects have benefited from the advent of dedicated project management offices, more powerful planning tools, and the growing importance of project management certification. On the other, IT projects continue to be plagued with problems that are decades old.

At the beginning of every project management workshop I've taught, I've conducted an informal survey of the kinds of problems faced by the organization's IT projects. Over the years, the results have shown a troubling set of nagging problems. You could even call them systematic in nature. Participants consistently list project management challenges such as: unreasonable or predefined due dates, lack of executive management support, inadequate resources, ill-defined or changing requirements, poor or shifting priorities, politics, and insufficient client participation.

The really sad part of the exercise is the litany of problems listed from the client's perspective. With stunning regularity, participants list problems like too much red tape and bureaucracy, IT-imposed solutions, missed deadlines, blown budgets, not being kept properly informed, and a failure to provide business benefit and value. Too often, IT projects epitomize Yogi Berra's wry observation, "This is like déjà vu all over again."

That's why it's so important for IT leaders to recognize that project management is not just a scientific endeavor comprising knowledge of tools and methodologies. There's an art to managing projects that requires a mindset I just don't see very often in companies across the country today.

Perhaps the best way to describe that mindset is to tell you about my background. I began my IT career 33 years ago as an EDP auditor in a bank. I was assigned to oversee the conduct and results of internal IT projects. In addition to making sure that the system being developed was well controlled, I was also charged with assessing if the process for building the system was well controlled. During my four years as an auditor, I witnessed project management behavior that varied from the truly accomplished and sublime to the kind of foolishness that bordered on professional incompetence.

I then transferred into a systems development department and quickly learned that the job of an IT project manager was challenging on the best of days. One fact became very clear: A project manager has a lot more responsibility than formal authority.

Fortunately, I had the opportunity to work with some outstanding project managers who impressed me with not only their technical capability but also their professional "charm." In the absence of authority, these project managers got things done by influencing their clients, team members, and project stakeholders. In other words, they relied on their ability to forge meaningful relationships and to act in an influential way. The concept of influence is so important it's covered in depth in Chapter 4, on consulting skills.

What I learned is that while techniques, tools, and technology are important, it's relationship-building and interpersonal skills that are essential to project management success. Years later, I still refer to the project management workshop I developed as "a three-day charm school for project managers."

Today, good IT leaders realize that successful project managers are those trained to master the human side of their projects, as much as the supporting tools and methodologies. They have learned that projects succeed for one reason and one reason only: because the people on the project succeed. That's right; even if the project team misses a target date or blows the budget, a project can still be successful if the client perceives that the team was responsive and competent and achieved the objectives of the project.

So much of what we do in IT is project-based. That's why, so far in this book, we've concentrated on mindsets and skills that indirectly contribute to enhanced project delivery. In this chapter, I dive into the heart of project management itself, focusing on how IT leaders can improve their organization's project success rate by changing their mindsets and improving how they structure, plan, and manage projects. Then, the following two chapters, continue on the project management theme by showing IT leaders how they can change their organization's approach to gathering business requirements (see Chapter 7) and navigating corporate politics (see Chapter 8).

The Building Blocks of Project Management

Let's start by looking more closely at the term *project management*. It really doesn't fairly describe the job at all, because in actuality, the management part of the job is the final phase of a three-phase process. In my project management workshop, I've distilled the job of a project manager down into a group of essential processes, and arranged them into three phases: structuring, planning, and managing (see Figure 6.1).

The first two phases—structuring and planning—should consume more of a project manager's time than the last phase. And none of the stages can be approached mechanically. From what I've seen, most project managers also need to

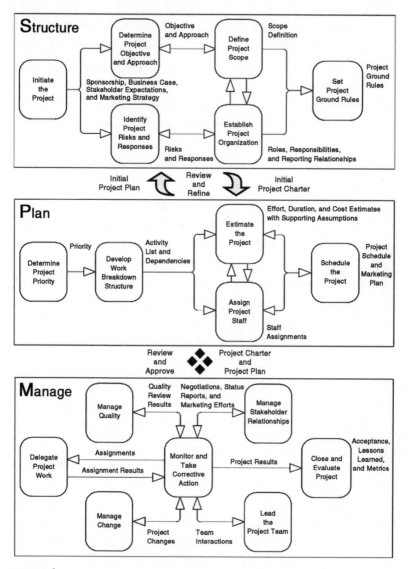

FIGURE 6.1 IT Project Management Essential Processes Map

undergo a mindset shift to focus on the real goal of any project: client satisfaction.

Imagine a homeowner having a pool built in his backyard. He hasn't done a lot of research into what size pool his lot will accommodate, how the excavator will get in, whether any water, sewer, electric, or cable lines will have to be rerouted, whether he wants a plaster or quartz interior, and so on. He's not thinking about his current landscaping being decimated during the digging process, the weather holdups, the debris scattered about his backyard while he waits for yet another subcontractor who fails to show up. He's just picturing himself and his family cannonballing into the refreshing water on a 90-degree day.

In order for this project to end in success, the pool company representative has a lot of upfront work to do, starting with structuring the project. His first task is to gain an appreciation for who in the family is the sponsor and who is the client. In our workshops, we prefer the term *client* to *sponsor,* if for no other reason than sponsor sounds so fiduciary in nature. We also believe that the concept of client orients the project to more of a service relationship versus a simple business transaction. And as any happy couple can attest, there can be a world of difference between dealing with the person who writes the checks and working with the person who has to be happy with the color of the tile.

Next, the pool rep has to work with this family of stakeholders on thinking about how they intend to use the pool—do they intend to swim laps, install a diving board, or float around drinking blender drinks? That might be called the project *objective.* Are they imagining an outdoor shower, lights, solar heater, spa, and a pool house? That's the project *scope.* Is there time in the schedule and money in the budget to do all of this? Will the homeowners' association approve the design? These are the *project constraints.* Do they understand what might happen when excavation begins (also known as *defining risk*), the type of communication they should expect, and when final payment is due (which is called *setting ground rules*)?

Only after completing this phase should the pool rep begin planning the project. This means breaking down the project into smaller parts and determining the order in which each piece should be accomplished (called the *work breakdown structure*), providing the homeowner with cost and time estimates, deciding which subcontractors to work with (also known as *assigning project staff*), and publishing a schedule that's accessible to everyone.

Finally, it's time to break ground. This involves making sure the excavation crew, concrete workers, plumber, electrician, and other workers understand what they're supposed to do (also called *work delegation*) and checking on their work to be sure it's up to snuff (known as *quality reviews*). But what if the excavators hit water? What if the pool's planned location doesn't leave enough room for the excavation equipment? What if equipment breaks down? What if the decking color doesn't come out right? For any of these glitches, the pool rep will need to negotiate schedule, budget, and design changes with the workers and the homeowner (called *change management* and *managing stakeholder relationships*). When the pool and landscaping are finally complete to the owner's satisfaction, it's time to close out the project, including a review of lessons learned and metrics that can be carried over into the next project.

Now imagine what would happen if the pool rep didn't do any of the upfront structuring and planning activities. The first obstacle to come along would likely result in one angry homeowner, thus setting up a rocky road for the entire duration of the project. In the end, the pool may get built, but at what cost? The only way the homeowner will deem the project a success is if he perceives the overall experience as mostly positive, and that depends in large part on the upfront time spent on defining, structuring, and planning.

And it's not just the structuring, planning, and management activities themselves that are important. During all this time that he's engaging with the homeowners, the pool rep is using a tool that IT people don't think about very much—his own personality and his ability to establish a relationship and even a rapport with the homeowners. Let's face it: Things can go wrong with any complex undertaking, and working through those obstacles is a lot easier when you have a strong partnership with the client.

And that's the real job of the project manager: developing a partnership with the project sponsor and key clients, involving them in structuring and planning the project, and then using well-honed project management techniques to see it through to completion.

Structuring Projects for Success

Now let's take a closer look at the individual building blocks of project management. Let's start with structuring.

The first job of a project manager is to take an assignment and turn it into a project. However, merely defining a project is not enough. Projects must be structured for success. The most crucial work in this project initiation phase is sponsor and client identification. Many of the problems associated with IT projects can be traced back to poor or nonexistent sponsorship. If the sponsor and client are not the same person, then it's vital that the project manager understand the role of each on the project.

For example, who provides the strategic direction for the project? Who is funding it? Who will benefit from it? Who will provide resources for it? Who will approve deliverables? Who can approve changes to the project? Who needs to know project status?

In the end, project initiation is the ultimate "moment of truth" for project managers. This first contact with the client sets the tone for the remainder of the project. It requires the utmost in tact and charm.

After initiation, the project manager continues project structuring by framing the project's business case and specifying business benefits, understanding project constraints, developing a solution strategy for the project, and determining its objective. It's important to mention that the project manager needs to have sufficient domain knowledge to be able to ask the right questions whose answers will frame the business case.

Once the objective is confirmed by the client, the project manager can set project scope. Project scope is defined as the suite of deliverables produced over the life of the project to prove that the objective was met. Simply put, the scope statement is a comprehensive list of what results are in and out of the project. As a quality assurance step, the project manager validates that the scope statement's list of deliverables is complete and sufficient to meet the project's objective.

Next, the project manager identifies project risks and possible mitigation strategies, and he establishes the project's organizational structure (roles, responsibilities, and reporting relationships). The final process in structuring is establishing the all-important ground rules for conducting the project. The results of project structuring are documented in the project charter.

Developing Plans that Work

The second phase in our three-phase approach is planning the project. While the perspective of structuring is *big picture* and strategic in nature, planning is detail oriented and tactical. For example, the essence of structuring is figuring out who are the key players on the project, what do they want, and why is it important to them. On the other hand, planning focuses on how and when it will be accomplished, as well as by whom.

Project planning begins with an understanding of the relative priority of the newly defined project work to everything else on the project manager's plate. Prioritization is the interplay between the urgency of the work (that is, the due date) and the value or importance of the work. Enterprises without good work prioritization processes often tend to spend their scarce and expensive IT staff on urgent work rather than important work. One of the hallmarks of an effective IT organization is its ability to focus talent on high-value work with laserlike precision.

Once a project manager has received clear marching orders, she can begin planning the project in earnest. The heart of project planning is developing a good understanding of the work to be done. The process is called developing a *work breakdown structure,* or WBS. A WBS is a purpose-built list of tasks to be accomplished on the project. The key to a good WBS is linking every task to a deliverable in the project charter's scope statement. Smart project managers will endeavor to involve team members in developing the WBS because this gives the people who will do the work some say in what work needs to be done. A well-defined WBS will make the next planning process—estimating the work—much easier.

An estimate is often referred to as an educated guess. The hard part is getting sufficiently educated about the project before the guessing begins. At O&A, our systematic approach to structuring and planning is intended to educate the people involved in estimating well enough to do a credible job.

There are many ways to estimate a project, including SWAGs, bottom-up, resident expert, analogous, and parametric. There is also an array of automated tools for estimating IT projects. Unfortunately, while most IT shops have planning and scheduling tools, many do not own or use estimating tools. In the absence of using estimating tools, my experience has shown Delphi or consensus-based estimating to work very well. A Delphi estimate draws on the collective experience of multiple estimators to develop a reasonable range estimate with supporting assumptions. Performed with knowledgeable participants in a consensus manner, a Delphi estimate is second only to estimating tools in its accuracy.

Staffing the project can occur in tandem with estimating. In fact it's a good practice to involve team members who will be doing the work in estimating the work. What I like to emphasize here is that the project manager needs to be involved in helping to select the team. Unfortunately, that's not often what happens; in fact, one of the most common complaints about staffing that I hear in my workshops is the project manager's lack of say over who will participate on the project. All too often, the only criterion for team membership is availability, and the critical process of staffing a project team ends up being a poor take on musical chairs. The haphazard formation of project teams speaks volumes about the perceived importance and value of teamwork within an organization.

The final process in developing a project work plan is scheduling the work. Once again, the importance of this effort is lost because of how it is often performed. A lot of project schedules are simply manufactured out of thin air. A specified due date is given, and the project manager endeavors to fit the project into the available time between the "when" and "now." The insidious nature of this form of reverse engineering turns the entire process of planning into a cruel joke. With so much "winking and nodding" going on, it's a miracle that whiplash is not a more common occurrence on IT projects.

Overall, though, we have to remember that the project plan is separate from the reality of doing the project. A good plan should lay out a reasonable and feasible approach to the project. However, it is a guide and, as such, will be subject to revision based on the reality of the work. Years ago, I had the pleasure of belonging to a Civil Air Patrol search and rescue organization. As part of briefing search pilots, we would constantly remind them that the map is not the terrain. The same holds true for projects—the plan is the map, not the terrain.

Regrettably, I have witnessed good project managers turning themselves into human pretzels trying to get reality to fit the plan. Such is not the way of the world.

Managing to Successful Completion

The final phase of our three-phase approach is managing the project. As shown from previous sections, O&A's approach places a lot of emphasis on preparation before execution. Now, with preparations completed, the real work can begin, as many of my workshop participants are eager to point out. I always find it striking how telling that comment is about a company's IT project culture.

Managing the actual work of a project involves seven subprocesses. The first three are interrelated and interactive processes that form the core of what I refer to as the essential *mechanics* of managing the work:

1. *Project delegation.* The first overt act of managing a project is delegation, or the process of getting the work off the plan and into the hands of the project team members. On the surface, delegation appears to be a mundane process, and it's true that during my career I've met many people who consider it a very pedestrian skill. However, most of these same people will also readily admit that they've been on the receiving end of poor delegation situations.

   In my workshops, we conduct an exercise to identify some of the reasons why project managers don't delegate very well. The reasons most often cited include ego, fear of conflict, fear of failure, (the petty) fear of success, "I can do it faster or better," ignorance, lack of authority, control problems, and trust issues. What's very illuminating about this exercise is that most participants recognize that the reasons they list are nothing more than excuses for not doing an important part of the project management job.

Time pressures often exaggerate the problem. What should be a thoughtful and collaborative process is all too often truncated into a perverse form of dumping on a team member. Regrettably, this can damage the relationship between the project manager and the team member.

2. *Managing quality.* The second interrelated process is managing quality. If a project manager is not actively ensuring the management of a high quality product, then what is he really managing? The approach I like to advocate is based on a traditional blend of defect prevention and defect detection. For example, I'm a strong believer in the benefits of conducting quality reviews, which are a visual inspection of any project deliverable, with the purpose of finding mistakes in that deliverable. People are generally very good at finding mistakes in other people's work, and smart project managers will capitalize on this very human tendency.

There's also a very important serendipitous aspect associated with the defect-detection job of doing reviews: A well-performed quality review, timed appropriately in the development life cycle, is also a very good defect prevention technique. A well-managed review process is the basis of all quality management and the essential precursor to all testing efforts. Results of the quality-review process provide the project manager with critical insight and input into the management function.

3. *Managing change.* The third interrelated process is managing change. It's a simple fact of life that change happens, especially on large IT-based projects. Change is inevitable and must be properly dealt with. The current crop of agile methodologies pride themselves on their advocacy of embracing change during systems development. This is not only a sound development practice, it's also a good management practice.

The focus of change management is to provide the client with a realistic assessment of the impacts associated with a requested change. Once clients understand the impacts, they can make an informed business decision regarding the acceptance, deferral, or rejection of the change. A good change management process will also provide the project manager with valuable insight into the dynamics of the project. The practice of leading change is so important that we've dedicated a chapter to it (see Chapter 11).

4. *Monitoring and taking corrective action.* The focal points of the three processes we've discussed so far are monitoring and taking corrective action. Monitoring—which involves the collection, analysis, and presentation of project performance data—is passive from the standpoint that it only provides the project manager with an understanding of project status. Taking corrective action—which requires the project manager to do something about the situation—is the active portion of the equation.

   During my tenure as an IT manager, the one quality I cherished the most in a project manager was a bias for action. My constant admonishment was, "Lead, follow, or get out of the way, but for the sake of the project, do something." I always preferred guiding a project manager versus having to build a fire under one. A perennial trick question in project management is, "How does a project get a year behind?" The answer, of course, is one day at a time. Therefore, the project must be actively managed every single day. There is no autopilot.

5. *Managing stakeholder relationships.* The next two processes are often regarded as the soft side of project management, but actually, experience has shown them to be the real hard work on a project. Managing stakeholder relationships is the underlying philosophy of O&A's overall approach to project management. The key relationship is between the project manager and his or her client. The building blocks of this relationship include the project manager's professional

competence, open and effective communications, a genuine interest in and understanding of the client and their business needs, and the demonstrated behavior of always acting in the best interest of the client.

While the relationship originates as part of the project assignment, it is fostered by the project manager's willing commitment to the assignment. It is first and foremost a service-based relationship with a complementary ethical obligation to act professionally on behalf of the client. Project stakeholders have two key indicators to gauge the quality of their relationship with the project manager. First, are they being kept suitably involved in the project? And second, are they being kept properly informed about its status? My colleagues have written at length about the consulting skills that project managers should employ (see Chapter 4), as well as the importance of building and engaging in a service-oriented mindset (see Chapter 3).

6. *Leading the team.* I purposely use the word *lead* rather than *manage* or *control*. Leadership extends both the client's and the project manager's sphere of influence beyond the mere administration of a project. Leadership by the client ennobles the project's objective. It raises the stakes, legitimizes the need, and changes the effort from a game to a cause.

One of the most powerful motivators for IT professionals is the opportunity to make a real difference in the business. It's truly regrettable that so few business clients leverage this powerful secret to project success. On the other hand, leadership by the project manager emboldens the actions of the team. Project teams thrive on being allowed (or empowered) to be creative, to experience the excitement of discovery, to enjoy a sense of real accomplishment, and to have fun while doing great things. Simply put, a good project manager can lead a project team to places it could never be driven to. We've discussed the qualities of leadership and how to make this transformation in Chapter 2.

One final point about motivation—motivation is not something a project manager does to a team member. Rather, it's something a team member does for herself. Motivation is a door that is locked from the inside. The best a project manager can do is create a climate that enables and encourages good work. The vast majority of IT professionals I've met in my career want to do a good job. It's truly unfortunate that far too many of them are forced into situations that discourage, inhibit, and on occasion penalize their best efforts. The key is to manipulate the environment, not the people.

7. *Close the project.* The last process in managing a project is to close and evaluate the project. The central activity of this process involves compiling lessons learned from the finished project and using them to form the basis of improvement recommendations. These improvements are directed at enhancing the enterprise's tools, methods, and procedures for future projects. This cycle is the driving force behind the continuously learning organization.

The final act of a project manager is to officially end the project. Win, lose, or draw, it's always good form to close down the effort on a gracious note—with a party if deserved, or a wake if warranted.

The Four Tenets of the Project Manager's Mindset

Now that we've discussed the four-phase approach to managing projects, we can turn our attention to something that's a little less tangible but just as important: Changing our staff's mindset toward project management.

Being a successful project manager requires more than just following project management methodologies, approaches, and metrics. It requires a fundamental change in the approach that most project managers take. If we allow our organizations to continue managing projects with their head in the wrong place, the chance of project success is nil. Here are four basic tenets that every project manager should internalize to better get their head into the project management game, in order of priority.

Tenet 1: Serve the Client

Being a project manager requires committing oneself to both the letter and spirit of the job. Project managers have typically been held to three accountabilities: on time, on budget, and according to requirements. I regard these as the letter portion of the job title. In essence, they're what project managers are paid to do.

But there's a fourth and—from what I see, often forgotten—accountability: client service. I consider this to be the spirit of the job. As an agent of the client, the project manager's job is to provide service and to provide it professionally, competently, and with the best interests of the client in mind. The aim of this tenet is client satisfaction. Technology may be the underlying mechanism, but it's not the purpose of the project. It is there to perform a job that the client needs to do.

So the number one job is serving the client by understanding their interests, their challenges, their relationships with others in the business, and their history. This requires a deft touch and a willingness to really listen and attempt to value the client's needs. After all, project managers can't provide good service if they don't know whom they're serving and why.

Some workshop participants have challenged me on this point by asserting that I must therefore believe that the client is always right. What I'm actually saying is that the client isn't always right, but they're always the client. Service requires giving respect and deference to the client's requirements and needs. At the same time, service is not servitude, and just doing everything the client says to is not providing a service. These concepts are so important that the topic of improving our organizations' service mentality is covered in Chapter 3.

Also, while the chief aim of this tenet is client satisfaction, the point isn't to achieve satisfaction at all costs. Sometimes, the greatest service you can perform for your client is to tell her that the current course of action is not in her best business interest, and to provide viable options. I refer to this as *adult dialogue,* and it should be revered on a project. In other words, don't accept whining, moaning, excuses, lies, or finger pointing. If you like what is happening on the project, say so. If you don't like what's happening, say so. Be genuine. No baggage, no games, no bullying. Engage in fear-free communication. Insist on hearing and telling the plain and simple truth. Demand personal accountability for quality work by everyone on the project. It's interesting to speculate how many project failures could have been averted if only the project manager had engaged the client in real adult dialogue.

Of course, not all clients are ready for this two-way relationship. For example, you might get a client who's not sufficiently knowledgeable or engaged. In this case, the project manager needs to educate the client on his role and responsibilities, how crucial it is for him to provide strategic direction, to help resolve political problems, make resources available, champion the cause to the enterprise, establish clear priorities—the things that only an executive sponsor can do. The project manager may also need to educate the client on this role, why it's crucial to do the upfront planning and structuring, to have a project charter, to engage in change management strategies, and so on.

The challenge for project managers is to create the kind of relationship with the client that makes these types of exchanges realistic and credible—which is not always easy when the client has significantly more power in the organization than they do. Let's face it: One of the biggest challenges for project managers is to have so little authority but so much responsibility for making the project succeed. This imbalance of power and how to navigate the resulting politics is discussed in Chapter 8, on managing politics.

Tenet 2: Accomplish the Mission

The second tenet revolves around the job of project management. Here's where the project manager brings her craft into play—all the work described earlier in the chapter. This is the technical work of project management, and clients should have a solid expectation that the project manager working with them is strong in her craft.

It's important to note that all the mechanical work involved with accomplishing the mission is secondary to serving the client. It's easy to get lost in the weeds of project management methodologies and tools and lose your focus on what you're really doing.

Tenet 3: Grow the Team

Note the use of the term *grow* rather than *develop*. Nurturing a good team is not an engineering project in which you assemble parts and pieces according to a prescribed series of processes. It's more akin to agriculture, where you start with good seeds, put them in fertile soil, provide them with water and sunlight, and—hopefully—get a good crop. But a good crop is not guaranteed; you can do all the right things, and the people you've assembled may still not gel as a team.

To maximize your chances, you need to make a conscious decision to work skillfully with the staff members you've selected. You need to solicit their ideas, create a collaborative environment, and provide a forum in which their best efforts can surface. The best environment in which to grow a team is one that's open and invites project team members to elevate issues and concerns. Your goal should be that at the end of a project, the people who've worked together are better for it— they've learned new things, applied their specialties, and shared their own worth and value with the enterprise.

Remember, people require lots of time. It's an oxymoron to believe that you can be efficient with the people on your project. Effectiveness as a project manager is born out of investing time in the wellbeing of the client, stakeholders, and team members. Taking care of the troops is not just a military truism. I have often been amazed, inspired, and even saved by the good works of my project team members. Take the time necessary to help ensure that your relationships with the people on your project are always in good repair. Then, be ruthlessly efficient with everything else.

You'll know you have a high performance, gelled team when you see the following characteristics:

- A shared elevating vision or goal
- A strong sense of team identity
- Mutual trust
- Interdependence among team members
- Open and effective communications
- A sense of autonomy
- Low turnover
- Joint ownership of the product
- A high level of obvious enjoyment

Of course, these are human beings we're talking about, and just like with raising kids, there are a limited number of ways to get it right and an infinite number of ways to get it wrong. That's why this third tenet is where many inexperienced project managers stumble, particularly with the increasing number of virtual teams, where members in different geographic regions meet by videoconferences and communicate by e-mail and phone. When team members never get the chance to meet, they may not even consider the importance of gelling and truly working as a team. They might easily adopt a contractor's mentality, in which they get the work done and move on. That will be an ongoing challenge to project managers trying to instill a sense of teamwork.

Notice that "growing the team" comes after "accomplishing the mission." Getting the work done is the priority, of course, and there are times when the necessity and urgency of the work takes preeminence. But let's face it—no one wants to get the mission accomplished on the backs of a broken and mangled staff.

Tenet 4: Own the Project

This last tenet is the enabler for all the others—the solid belief on the part of the project manager that he has a personal stake in the outcome of the project. I have come to regard project management as the courageous application of common sense in uncommon situations. But where does the courage come from if not from the genuine belief that our good name will be associated with the results of the project? The success or failure of the project reflects on the project manager, and that personal aspect is important. If the project manager doesn't have a sense that he is on the line—that the project doesn't reflect his talents and abilities—then he won't be able to make the hard calls that a project often demands.

For example, without a strong personal stake in the project, how can you find the courage to tell a client that what she is doing is not in the best interests of the business? Or deal with a team member whose performance is below par? Or confront a vendor that's not doing its job? Without a sense of ownership, it's pretty easy to slough off responsibility, overlook shoddy work, and dismiss dysfunctional behavior. The project manager's attempts at championing the project will ring hollow, and the team will see through it in a minute.

This strong personal identity with the project is not the same as the sponsor's ownership of the product. The sponsor truly owns the project deliverables because she paid for them. A personal sense of ownership by a project manager does not, in any way, absolve the client of her responsibilities as client.

It's also important to note that project managers' ownership should not be construed to mean that IT is taking over the project. Organizational sourcing of the project management role should have no effect on the professional obligation to act as the client's agent and not as the boss.

Conclusion: Thinking like a Project Manager

Project management is truly a blend of both art and science. But that's not widely understood in our industry. From what I see in companies throughout the United States today, IT professionals focus way too much on the tools, methodologies, and other mechanical aspects of project management. And by going so far out there in the weeds, they often lose sight of why they're managing all these projects in the first place: to create systems that satisfy the real needs and requirements of the clients who depend on them.

I'm not saying that project managers don't need to know their craft. In fact, knowing the mechanics of structuring, planning, and managing projects is absolutely essential, which is why I build workshops around these very important building blocks of the job.

However, managing a project is not a purely mechanical endeavor. The difference between project successes and failures is how those skills are applied, and the secret ingredient is the project manager's own mindset. When you overlay a solid understanding of project management essentials with a mindset of satisfying the client, that's a recipe for success.

It's really a matter of staying focused on these essentials and trying to avoid boiling the ocean. I had the unfortunate experience of working for a manager who constantly tried to do too much. Nothing was good enough. Every minor slip or shortfall was treated as a capital offense. He meddled, nagged, and bemoaned every action taken on the project. It was not only exhausting and highly unprofessional, but it was in large measure unnecessary to the success of the project. I believe there are just six areas of focus on most projects:

1. Pay attention to the schedule
2. Mind the budget
3. Manage the scope
4. Monitor the quality
5. Foster your relationship with your client
6. Attend to your team

That's pretty much it; most everything else is just noise.

In short, project managers won't succeed by memorizing the latest techniques and immersing themselves in the methodology of the day. It's a job that requires positive relationships and total engagement with people.

Top Ten

Tenets for Managing Projects

10. Manage the work, not the plan.
9. Deal only with reality—insist on seeing results, not just being told about them.

(continued)

(*continued*)

8. Projects don't go from great to awful overnight; it happens one day at a time.

7. Bad news doesn't age well. Keep your client, stakeholders, management, and team members informed.

6. MBWA—Manage by Wandering Around (with credit to Tom Peters, *In Search of Excellence*.) If you want to know what's going on, get up out of your cube and go look at it.

5. Be efficient with things but effective with people.

4. Pace is not the same as progress—provide time for people to catch their breath and celebrate their successes.

3. Stay focused; don't try to boil the ocean.

2. Insist on adult behavior from everyone on the project.

1. Earn the privilege to be regarded as the project manager every day.

Specific Actions I Will Take

-
-
-

CHAPTER 7

Changing Your Requirements-Gathering Mindset

The success of any IT project is determined at the very beginning of the project life cycle, when the IT staff meets with business clients to gather requirements. But IT's track record with this important phase is similar to its history with project management itself: abysmal. Requirements have been gathered for decades, but most IT organizations have yet to discover a consistently successful way of sitting down with business clients, discussing their needs, and translating those needs into a useful system, enhancement, customization, or software package selection.

In fact, according to some statistics, poor requirements gathering is the cause of about 70 percent of today's technology project failures. That's because passing along one bad requirement is akin to throwing a stone into a pond and watching how far the ripples go. According to some calculations, each badly defined requirement results in 10 bad design statements, which then can multiply out to 100 incorrect coding statements. Even if that's an exaggeration, you can easily see how poor requirements negatively affect application integrity, maintenance costs, and client satisfaction. This is true whether you're looking to build a custom system, buy a new software package, or enhance an existing system.

Skipping requirements gathering is like building a house without a plan. For example, I've seen companies buy software that didn't meet their business needs, mainly because they wanted to save time on the requirements step. When they tried to modify the package to meet their needs, they discovered they didn't know the requirements. Sadly, they concluded that the step they skipped really did need to be done to make the package useful.

I often see organizations turn to yet another vendor tool or methodology in their attempt to improve this situation. But just like with project management, IT is facing a problem that requires less of a scientific fix and more of a mindset change—a change that emphasizes the upfront work of really communicating with business clients to discover what they need.

From what I've seen in my 24 years in the IT profession and from working with clients across the country, this is a mindset change that's way past due, as business leaders grow increasingly frustrated with the disconnect between what clients need and what IT delivers. I learned about the importance of good requirements throughout my varied IT career, which included stints in analysis, development, production support, project management, and relationship management. It became clear to me that to have success in any of these roles, it all starts with good requirements. Everyone who has to read and use them appreciates them, they increase productivity and quality, and they add accountability. And lastly, a good requirement is measurable because either the end product delivers on that requirement, or it doesn't.

Specifically, I learned two critical things about gathering requirements:

1. Always figure out and then describe *what* the problem is and always state *what* is needed, because there are many solutions to a given problem.

2. Don't come up with a solution before you know what the requirements are. There are just too many people who want to tell you how to do your job.

How many times has your IT staff rushed through the client interview stage to jump in to what they consider to be the real work of designing and programming? And when they do spend time with clients, are they really listening? Or are they busy trying to relate what they hear to something they're already familiar with, like another system they've recently built or a platform they're comfortable with? Other times, they might hear just a little bit and immediately determine that what clients want simply can't be done, instead of asking more questions to verify their understanding.

To better understand the problem, imagine you're a bridge designer, and a client comes to you, describing his need to get over a body of water so he can cross from one landmass to another separate piece of land. You'd start designing a bridge, right? Well, what if you were in the submarine business? Or the airline industry? Or a tunnel engineer? The point is, the client simply needs to get from one piece of land to the other, and whether that's best done by bridge, submarine, balloon, or dirigible can only be determined by an unbiased third party who knows how to unlock the client's real needs and expectations. How many times a day does the client need to go back and forth? How quickly does he expect to be able to accomplish it? How many other people need to do the same thing? Do they all have to move at the same time?

And it's not as though business clients are any better at this. In fact, today's more technology-savvy clientele often come to IT with a solution based on a recent article they've read or a conference they've attended. Then, the IT staff feels it's up to them to implement that solution rather than backing up and finding out what the client's real needs are.

No tool or methodology can resolve these problems. It's a matter of changing the IT organization's mindset and helping them develop new skills so they can see things through the eyes of the client, establish a rapport, ask the right questions, actively listen to the responses, ensure understanding, and accurately translate those needs into a written document. And keep in mind that the ability to quickly and effectively capture, validate, and control client requirements doesn't just apply to project managers and business analysts. These are essential survival skills for anyone working in today's IT environment of lean staffing and crunch-mode projects.

When IT leaders become more aware of the skills gaps that exist in their own organizations, they can transform their organization's requirements-gathering culture and help individuals develop the needed skill sets, independent of any particular vendor's tool or methodology. When they affect this type of change, the results can be astounding. I know—I've seen it. Recently, I worked with a client who had two project teams that were trained to do requirements gathering. The first team adapted the techniques the second team did not. The first team delivered their project on time and on schedule, with high client satisfaction. Their clients, geographically dispersed, were enthusiastic about how well the project team understood their needs and communicated their progress. The second team was over budget, behind schedule, and constantly heard complaints from their clients. To paraphrase one of the client responses, "We don't know what we're getting or when."

The *What,* Not the *How*

I think of the requirements-gathering process as a journey, with plenty of precarious twists and unexpected turns along the way. If you're a skillful driver, you can stay on track and arrive at your destination. But poorly negotiating the curves or taking a wrong turn can result in a lot of wandering along unpaved roads that lead nowhere. Unfortunately, a successful arrival requires a skill set that—from what I've seen in my work with IT organizations— most IT professionals don't have. It's the job of the IT leader to not only become familiar with the optimum route to requirements-gathering success but also to teach their staffs how to navigate.

The first and most important skill is steering the client interview toward what I call the *what*, not the *how*. From the hundreds of projects I've worked on, I can say that this is the biggest downfall of most IT professionals. In their zeal to get to what they consider *real* IT work, many project managers and business analysts start shaping the solution to the client's needs (the how) before they really understand what those needs are in the first place (the what). But as soon as they do this, it's a guarantee that they're veering from the right path.

Let me explain it this way. Do you have any 8- to 12-year-olds in your life—a neighbor, a niece or nephew, a son, or daughter? If so, you may have heard them say how much they need, really need, a cell phone. But have you ever asked them what they intend to do with this electronic device they seemingly can't live without? If so, you've probably heard answers like, "Talk to my friends" (have you ever been on the other end of an 8-year-old's phone conversation?), "Let my parents know where I am" (how far do 10-year-olds really travel these days?), or more likely, "Download a cool ring tone." By pressing further, you might uncover that it's not really a cell phone your young tweener friend really needs at all and that what she is really after is a sense of independence, of feeling like a grown-up, of keeping up with the latest technology rage—all things that can be achieved in a variety of ways and not necessarily with a cell phone (which they're bound to lose or at least lose interest in after showing it off for a few days).

Thankfully, talking with clients is usually not like talking with a 12-year-old, but the common thread is that you can't automatically assume that the solution clients say they need is really the optimum one. Arriving at that requires digging underneath the surface, steering the client toward describing not how they want something built but what they need to accomplish. Remember, your goal is to figure out what the client needs from the new system or modification or software package—not how he or she wants it to be built or designed. In other words, project managers, business analysts, and others need to learn to leave the how to the designers and consider their job to be getting to the what.

To understand this better, let's go back to the bridge example. If someone comes up to you and says, "There's a river over there. Can you build me a bridge?"; that's a how. But if you ask the person, "What do you need to do? What is your goal?" she might answer, "I need to get to the other side." That's the what. And when you get to the what, you realize there are many options for the how, whether it's a bridge, a tunnel, a ferry, or a submarine. In other words, you don't want to design the answer; you just want them to tell you what they really want. There can be many solutions and many designs to fit the client's needs, and that should be left to the designers to figure out, not the requirements gatherers.

By asking what instead of short-circuiting the process by starting with the how, you can air out many other designs and approaches, some of which might be better than the how the client comes to you with.

A typical example from my experience is a client bringing me a screen or a report with a new column added and saying, "This is what I want!" By questioning what the client needs with the column, I might find that the information is derived; for example, formulas need to be defined, *the data don't exist anywhere in IT* (it's on a client's spreadsheet), or the information is readily available somewhere else, like in *another report or application not currently used by the client.*

126

I was working with an IT organization that related the following example of falling into the how trap. Their business client came to them with modified screenshots showing how they needed the system to be changed. The IT organization worked with the client to spec out the changes and sent it offshore for development. When the newly modified screens were returned for testing, someone in the IT organization asked why a new set of screens was developed to handle functionality that already existed! It turns out that the business client was unaware that the functionality existed, and the existing functionality would work just fine.

The Importance of the Interview

The next fork in the road that can throw requirements gatherers off course is the mistake of taking client requests at face value. Far too many IT organizations take on the role of order taker—listening to what clients want and unquestioningly delivering to spec—only to discover the final result doesn't serve the business needs at all. This is such an easy trap for IT professionals to fall in to that it was discussed in more depth in Chapter 4, on consulting skills.

Simply put, clients don't always know how to communicate their needs, and it's now up to IT to lead the way. And the way to do that is by developing strong interview skills, which is yet another Achilles' heel for many IT professionals. From what I see in the IT organizations I work with, most IT staffs approach the client interview as a check-off item to complete as quickly as possible rather than as an opportunity to build rapport, establish a partnership, and really understand what the business is trying to accomplish. It's the IT leader's job to sensitize the IT staff to the importance of the interview and teach them how to take advantage of this prime time with the client.

Good interviews don't just happen. It's good to ask a lot of questions, but you don't want to come across as disrespectful or annoying. It's important to steer the client toward talking about what he wants, but you don't want to appear arrogant or negative. There are many fine lines that need to be walked, and the only way for the IT staff to keep its balance is to develop communication skills.

One of the most common interview problems I see is when the interviewer becomes frustrated with the interviewee, especially when he thinks the interviewee doesn't know anything. I have heard statements such as, "Can I talk to X, who knows something about the request/problem," without realizing that she has just insulted the person she is addressing (usually management).

First and foremost, a satisfying interview requires establishing a rapport with the person or people with whom you're partnering, which means allowing the conversation to naturally flow beyond a discussion of work and technology. Such camaraderie will go far when you inevitably run into conflicts, confrontations, and other difficult conversations with the client in the future. The idea of establishing rapport is so important that we've also discussed it in Chapter 4 on consulting skills and Chapter 8 on politics.

For the purposes of requirements gathering, however, there are some specific ways to open the lines of communication. One idea is to encourage the IT organization to conduct their interviews in the client's office, which will help set the client at ease. This is important because an intimidated or defensive client won't be inclined to open up to the requirements gatherer. This also gives the IT professional the chance to look around the office for personal mementos such as photographs that reveal something about the client's personality or life outside of work. These are easy conversation starters that can encourage a natural flow of communication that will benefit the IT staff when it gets down to the business at hand.

Because it doesn't come easily to many IT professionals, they need to be encouraged to ask about the client's golf game, his whitewater rafting trip, her marathon training, and listen for interests that they share. Such tidbits can be used for further conversation starters when IT professionals see the client again in the hallway or at their next meeting. Most people enjoy talking about themselves to people who seem truly interested, and that's what establishes human connections.

And last but not least, it is estimated that 55 percent of communication is nonverbal. I remember being in a client's office when IT called to get some information. The client said, "Okay" but rolled his eyes, frowned, and let out a groan. The caller heard, "Okay," but to anyone present in the office, there was obviously an issue that needed to be discussed and resolved.

Do note, though, that if an individual on the IT staff doesn't feel capable of engaging in this type of rapport, it's probably better for her to try another tack, like talking about the weather or something else of general human interest. The last thing you want is for her to come across as a phony who ritualistically asks the same question about the same photograph with no genuine interest in the client's answers. Similarly, if the client's office reflects nothing personal, that should be taken as a cue to the person's more bottom-line-oriented personality, in which case the IT staff should stick to the business at hand, such as asking, "How are sales?" or, "How's business?"

Another common interview mistake is for requirements gatherers to fail to establish a common language between themselves and the client. IT needs to be sensitized to understanding that, first, there is, indeed, a difference in terminology in the two worlds, and second, they need to be proactively encouraged to adopt the terminology of the business client. They can't be too proud to ask for definitions—acronyms in one industry can mean something else entirely in another industry, *or even in another division of the same company!* Problems occur when you persist in using the jargon of your own world or when you assume you understand the client's terminology.

In fact, you may discover that different business clients are using different words to mean the same thing. In those cases, the IT staff can serve as a bridge between clients, encouraging them to agree to a uniform vocabulary for a particular project or initiative and clearly defining that vocabulary in a project glossary or dictionary. When everyone is on the same page with their terminology, it eliminates a lot of room for confusion.

I have also come across the same acronym that means two different things depending on which business area of the company I'm working with. Since IT deals with the entire company, this leads to confusion when team members change, or requirements are passed on to designers. Not to mention the issues it causes for new hires, contractors, and offshore developers.

Here are some additional tips on helping the IT organization improve its interview success.

- *Take a who and what inventory.* Chances are that multiple clients will need to be interviewed, so it would be wise for the requirements gatherer to do some research ahead of time as to what pieces of information are needed and who's the most likely source for that information. For each person she interviews, she should know her objective. She doesn't, for example, want to waste someone's time talking about general ledger concerns if that's not that person's area of work.
- *Make a written list of questions.* This will help the requirements gatherer manage his time during the interview. He may arrive with ten questions, but if the person turns out to be a treasure trove of information, it might take half an hour to get the answer to the first one. If he still has nine to go, he can determine, in partnership with the client, whether they want to move on or plan another meeting.
- *Stay in an asking mode.* If the requirements gatherer concentrates on asking questions rather than making statements

or not responding at all, she'll avoid two common errors that I see IT professionals make: making assumptions and forming arguments. If she has even a shadow of a doubt about whether she understands something, she should ask for clarification or otherwise check her understanding. It's better to play stupid than misunderstand. And if she doesn't agree with something the client says, she should respond with a question. She's not there to argue; she's there to find out what the client needs.

- *Provide prototypes.* A good way to verify mutual understanding is to use visual aids, such as mock screens, reports, or models. It's important for the requirements gatherer to emphasize to the client, however, that the prototype is not the end product and is simply a tool to ensure that everyone's on the same page. Too often, when the IT staff draws a mock screen, the client is surprised when the actual screen doesn't turn out that way. One way to avoid this is to never leave the prototypes behind with the client.

- *Craft a smooth ending.* When ending the interview, the requirements gatherer should make sure he recaps his understanding of what he heard in the interview, explain the next steps, and express appreciation for the person's time.

Communicating through Pictures

A third wrong turn that I often see IT professionals make along the requirements-gathering path is to begin writing up the requirements before ensuring that she and the client are on the same page. All too often, after the client interview, the requirements gatherer disappears, sometimes for weeks, writes up the requirements, and then presents a fully written document to the client for feedback. When the client finally gets back to the IT professional—usually after a lengthy time lag—with changes, the process repeats itself, stretching out the back-and-forth review period for several months, with many lengthy lulls. At one company, requirements documents get rewritten an average of seven times before they reach final-copy stage! This approach is time consuming and absurd, and in the end, the chances of getting it right are slim to none.

Note that this is not what an iterative approach should look like. A healthy iteration means the work is being done, reviewed with users and quickly corrected in hours or days and repeated until the document is correct or complete. That's different from writing a full-length document, publishing it and tweaking it over a period of months.

To achieve that, I suggest inserting a picture-drawing phase into the process before jumping into the document-writing phase. Call them models, context diagrams, event analyses, or anything you wish—the idea is to create a clear communication tool that's easy for both IT and the client to see how everything connects and what's in and out of scope.

I've seen this method work on numerous occasions. In one case, a senior IT vice president had bought a software package to replace an existing antiquated application. He thought it solved the business needs and would be easy to install. There were no requirements. The development team was certain that the project would be a failure but was unable to communicate that upward.

Within an hour, we drew a context diagram to show all the system interfaces that needed to be developed to communicate with the new package. There were 57 system interfaces that would need to be designed, developed, and tested, and this did not include installing the package, loading the data, or ensuring the package met the client's needs.

Two hours later, after reviewing the context diagram, the senior vice president canceled the project, saying he didn't realize how big an effort it was to install and that we would need to get the requirements done before purchasing a new package.

A picture on one page communicated what the developers had been trying to tell management for two months!

In another case, I was involved in a large IT effort to build a new regulatory business process. We used modeling to first define the existing processes, and then modified the existing processes to accommodate the new process.

The first day was difficult, as the clients couldn't understand why we were drawing pictures and not writing requirements. But by Day 2, they had begun to fully utilize the modeling approach, with comments such as, "Take process X, modify this, this, and this, and it will do what we need to do." We were also able to establish and document a common business language definition.

Because most people can draw or model more quickly than they can write, this new step effectively minimizes the lull between initial interviews and the feedback loop, which keeps the discussion fresh and as close to real time as possible. Also, most people are more responsive to pictures and diagrams than a wordy document, which makes it easier to pull clients into a two-way, engaging conversation versus the arm's-length, removed, and disconnected type of communication that written documents promote.

Diagrams also make it easier for clients to see and explain what's wrong or missing in the system or process IT has modeled versus long, written documents. In fact, with longer documents, by the time many clients and IT staff get partway through them, they can barely remember what they read in the first half. But with a picture, IT can walk through the diagram with the client and discuss what's right and wrong.

If the IT staff does a good job with the initial interview and the iterations that follow from the picture-drawing stage, they'll find that when they actually write the requirements document, they'll end up revising it once or twice at most. That's because everybody involved has bought in to the ideas and thoughts behind the document, used a common language, and have given their feedback up front.

A word of warning: You may see so much success with picture drawing that you're tempted to go right to the prototyping phase, without writing a requirements document, or perhaps writing requirements only for business logic. However, this is a dangerous approach. While I have seen IT management push the idea of skipping written requirements, the risk is significant. Consider how vulnerable you'd be if key staff left the organization because of turnover, or a decision is made to offshore development. The lack of written requirements is a production support nightmare, not to mention when enhancements are requested. Also, without an agreed-upon set of requirements, there is no baseline established to manage change.

Writing a Solid Requirements Document

As we near the end of the requirements-gathering journey, there's still another fork in the road that can throw IT professionals off the path: writing the actual requirements document. Let's go back to the points made at the very beginning of this chapter. Since requirements are what designers use to design, testers use to test, and so on, one mistake in the requirements document has a negative ripple effect, plus we end up delivering something that doesn't fill the client's needs. We end up with patchwork new applications, with a high level of post-implementation defects, low client satisfaction, requests for enhancements, budget and schedule overruns—and that's if we succeed!

The goal is to write a simple document that is clear and concise. It should be easily understood by IT and the business, from senior management to the staff, with no ambiguity. I once worked for a CIO who said, "If I can understand it, then you've done a great job of writing the requirements." In other words, write it for someone who doesn't know what needs to be done.

So, in writing the requirements document, it's important to hold the power of words in the highest esteem, especially with something that requires the language precision that requirements documents do. This is where the rubber meets the road, and it's important for requirements writers to be as accurate as they possibly can, which again requires learning some new skills, this time based around written communications.

There are several language tricks you can pass along to requirements writers to ensure precision in the document. Here are two:

1. *The power of* Must. One is to make ample use of the word *must*. Must is one of the most powerful words in the English language, because when we use it, there are no two ways about the statement you're making. "X must do Y," plain and simple, 100 percent of the time, no exceptions. It's not the same with words like *should* and *shall,* which imply there's an undefined *maybe* out there, an unnamed exception to the rule. Those gray areas are exactly what lead writers of requirements documents into trouble.

   Unlike its cousins *should* and *shall, must* exposes the exceptions and forces people to define them. When clients read a must statement, they're likely to respond, "No, actually, that shouldn't happen under these specific conditions." This helps us capture what's so easy to miss—the exceptions to the rule.

   It's just a fact of life that many times, when you say, "X must do Y," someone will find an exception, even if it's as hidden as, "except when there's a blue moon following the harvest moon on the fifth month of an odd year." And those are the things that all too often just don't make it into the code.

Here's an example. At one company, a project team wrote a document with zero defects traced back to the requirements phase. That's because through computer modeling, 37 defects were exposed, all of which were instances in which each shall was changed to a *must*. When these changes were brought to the client, eight statements were flagged as having multiple exceptions.

2. *Watch out for* And. Another word to watch is *and*. As much as you can, try to eliminate any stray *and*s from your document, because their presence indicates that you've combined two thoughts that should be separate from each other. The whole idea is to keep the statements simple, and when it comes to designing code for the statements, it will be much easier if the designer understands there are two distinct thoughts, not two thoughts rolled into one.

Requirements need to be expressed in short, simple sentences with their associated exceptions. Way too often, I see one-sentence paragraphs that describe multiple requirements, which confuses everyone involved.

Conclusion

If IT professionals want to improve their project success rate, the first place to look is at the very beginning of the project life cycle: the requirements-gathering phase. This is not a phase to speed through and check off as soon as possible; it's an opportunity to establish a partnering relationship with the client and use all the communication skills you can muster to truly understand what the client needs.

For years, organizations have tried and failed to improve their requirements-gathering process, using the new tools being promoted or the methodology of the day. But despite all their efforts, they find themselves running into the same brick wall, falling down, and wondering yet again why they can't get it right.

That's why some IT leaders are beginning to try something different. They're setting upon the path of establishing a new mindset among their organizations to approach their projects differently and embark on the requirements-gathering journey with their compasses pointed in the right direction. With the right skills in hand, they can navigate the winding path and take all the right turns.

When you help your staff grow their communication and interpersonal skills, they become more insightful interviewers. It's only then that IT will stop building expensive bridges to nowhere and start helping their clients walk on water.

Top Ten

Techniques for Changing Your Requirements-Gathering Mindset

10. Establish rapport.
9. Communication is the key.
8. Interview the right people.
7. Talk in the business language and use pictures (models).
6. Don't assume—ask.
5. Don't solve the problem before you know what it is.
4. Requirements are short, concise sentences.
3. Use the power of *must*—exceptions will kill you.
2. *What* is a requirement, not *how*.
1. Give the people *what* they want.

Specific Actions I Will Take

-
-
-

CHAPTER 8

Sharpening Your Political Savvy

Many IT professionals view politics as something nasty. They'd rather resist, avoid, or ignore politics all together. Intrigue, power plays, control tactics, conflict—what does this have to do with managing technology? "Who me?" you might hear an IT professional say. "Leave it to others to battle for control and struggle for power. My job is to implement the technology solution."

But the fact is, where there's technology, there's change, and where there's change, there will be people who perceive themselves as winners and as losers. That's where politics begin. So, you can bury your head in the sand and ignore politics—and then you won't have to watch IT projects, the organization's reputation, and your own career go down the drain! The plain fact is, corporate politics aren't just for business clients anymore.

But they never really were. In fact, whether you've been aware of it or not, navigating politics has been a required skill for IT professionals—and particularly for project managers—ever since this field became a viable profession. And I should know—I've got the scars to prove it. I spent many years managing IT projects during my career. As a project manager, I found myself ensnared in more politically charged situations than I care to admit. I encountered resistance from business clients who were suspicious about the changes being forced upon them. I was embroiled in power struggles between departments.

I failed to get support from people I didn't even know were key to my project. I was robbed of resources by others higher up the organizational food chain who inserted their pet projects ahead of my own. My projects were getting hurt, and so was my reputation as a project manager.

My excuse for the project problems was that they were political—and politics wasn't my job. But standing by helplessly while my projects were derailed was frustrating for me and damaging to my future. Saying it wasn't my fault was not an effective promotion strategy!

And the plain truth is that it *was* my fault. Not because I created the political problems, but because I did nothing to manage them. Admittedly, I wasn't the fastest learner, but over time, I realized I couldn't afford to stand by helplessly. Reluctant clients, warring business departments, unsupportive higher-ups—these things were creating serious wounds that could kill my career. I eventually realized I could deal with all of these factors if I paid attention to the political influences around me. So I got my head out of the sand and worked to understand project politics and improve my own political skills.

Having learned a few things the hard way, I created the Politics of IT Project Management workshop for O&A a few years ago. I thought I could help other project managers avoid some of the bruises I got in the School of Hard Knocks. Nothing like it existed at the time, despite the fact that becoming politically savvy is absolutely essential to succeeding in this profession.

While political savvy is an essential skill for all levels of the IT organization, it's particularly crucial for project managers. Project managers have no authority over the business clients they work with, but they have plenty of responsibility to shepherd projects to completion. So in lieu of positional power, project managers need to learn the art of persuasion, influence, trust building, and rapport—in essence, political skills—to get the resources they need.

Unfortunately, resources are scarce in any corporation. Even in good times, there's never enough money, time, and people to do everything everyone wants to do. That means we're in competition with others for the resources we need to successfully complete our projects. Competition leads to internal conflicts. And since most corporations don't have thorough procedures to rationally allocate resources, the two means for resolving those conflicts are negotiations (discussed in Chapter 5) and politics.

So what is politics, anyway? Used negatively, politics is "intrigue or maneuvering within a group in order to gain control or power." You know it when you see it: It's the business client who just won't show up at your meetings. It's the divisional manager who refuses to accept the new corporate-standard accounting system. It's the sales department that insists it should have a major say in the development of the new procurement system. Negative politics divides people and disrupts progress.

But when used in a positive way, politics can bring people closer together. Positive politics is a legitimate activity to allow people with different interests to work out a collective purpose—and then work together to make it happen.

Picturing Yourself as a Political Player

To succeed at politics, IT professionals need to see themselves as political players. But many IT professionals don't have a clear picture of what it means to be politically savvy. So it might be easier to picture yourself navigating through a political situation outside of work. Consider this situation: You dropped off the lunch your child forgot to take to school this morning, and you see vending machines full of junk food around the cafeteria. Maybe you think the school's food policy should be changed to encourage healthier eating habits. What would be the first action you'd take? Would you storm into the principal's office and tell her she should be taking better care of the students?

More likely, you'd check with some teachers you've come to trust, to understand the history surrounding the development of the school's food policy. How long has it been in place, and has anyone tried to change it before? Perhaps you'd talk with other parents first to gauge their reaction to your concerns. Maybe you'd even drum up some support and even excitement around the issue. Is there a school newsletter, local newspaper, or parent blog? Maybe you'd get people discussing these issues through one of those media outlets.

You might even engage in some detective work: What are other schools doing about these issues? How long has the principal worked at this particular school, and what has been her previous reaction to suggested change? Does the principal prefer to talk by phone, e-mail, or meet face to face? Is there a group of teachers that seems to influence the principal more than others?

Clearly, your best chance to change things is through discovering the invisible influences—the internal politics—in the organization, and then playing your cards with those forces in mind.

And that's as true for the workplace as it is in a school, a neighborhood, or a volunteer organization. Where there are people—particularly people who sense that their stability, their beliefs, and their overall security are at stake—there are politics. And where there is a technology initiative, there is change— change that will enflame those politics like a spark ignites gasoline.

IT and Politics: Historically Strange Bedfellows

My brother-in-law managed a large sales territory for his company for 30 years. Harry knew that political savvy and awareness was critical to sales success. Any sales manager, vice president of finance, or divisional manager will tell you that—they grow up understanding it throughout their entire corporate lives.

That's one of the biggest problems IT professionals have—everyone else in the corporation understands this stuff, and they've been left out of the loop. Worse, business people can't even fathom that IT doesn't consider corporate politics and are left to wonder why they're handling these everyday situations so badly. When I told Harry I was developing a workshop to help project managers understand politics, he was surprised. "Why wouldn't they know that stuff already?" he questioned. Because nobody told them it was important! Think of all the training you've had on your way to becoming an IT leader—did anyone warn you to look over your shoulder for the political problems technology projects might ignite, let alone coach you on how to proactively ensure they don't flare out of control?

It's easy to believe that because technology projects are designed to improve work processes that everyone in the company will happily jump on board. But the reality is, technology projects always mean change, which is a threat to the status quo. As a result, there will always be a group of people who consider themselves the winners, as well as their counterparts, who perceive themselves as the losers. And while the winners make natural allies of IT and can be our best project champions, the losers will do everything they can to preserve and protect their territory. Unfortunately, those actions, either directly or inadvertently, could very well sabotage the project.

This is particularly true on the highly strategic, cross-divisional, and even global projects that many companies are embarking on today. More and more projects are being launched with the intent of breaking down traditional silos and creating synergies among disparate parts of the business. In fact, it's fair to say that the degree of damaging politics that IT professionals can expect to encounter is in direct correlation with the visibility of the project and the variety of stakeholders involved.

In my project manager days, I was once approached by the CFO of a fast-growing company that had recently acquired several other businesses. He had a problem: With all the different financial systems in use, it was taking six weeks to close the books. The CFO wanted to standardize on a single application to improve speed and efficiency.

We set up a project team and worked with the corporate financial group to choose the right application and began testing it. Everything went so well that the CFO wanted to immediately install the new system in the first field division.

When I walked into the general manager's office of the targeted field division, I was shocked when the manager was less than pleased to see me. "We've heard what you've been doing at corporate," the general manager barked, "and I don't know why you even bothered coming out here. We run our business our way, and we've got a guarantee of autonomy directly from the CFO. Our financial system works just fine for us, and we're not going to change it."

I was a victim of politics, right? But it didn't have to be that way. What if, instead of being blind-sided, I had looked at the big picture before even agreeing to take on the project? Shouldn't I have considered the needs, goals, and desires of the key stakeholders, in this case, the general managers of the field divisions? What if I had asked the CFO whether everyone was on board with the standardization effort—instead of assuming that they'd be fine with all the changes it entailed, not to mention the loss of some of their autonomy? Then perhaps I could have said that I'd be happy to lead this system change after the CFO had taken the appropriate organizational readiness steps. And if the CFO was unwilling to do that, it would have been a real clue of the political hot water that awaited me.

Very likely, the CFO knew exactly what he was doing— putting IT into the position of playing the bad guy that forces conformance through a system change rather than the CFO doing it himself. It's often a rude awakening for IT professionals to discover that the C in a C-level position doesn't always stand for organization-wide clout.

Clearly, career success will come to those who stop blaming politics and start handling them. Using politics as an excuse will no longer cut it when it comes to advancing the reputation and effectiveness of IT.

Politically savvy project managers can:

- Get their projects bumped up on the priority list.
- Cut through red tape.
- Get greater recognition.
- Get management buy-in on their projects.
- Get more project budget.
- Get the people they need—when they need them.
- Get their ideas heard.
- Bring projects to successful conclusions.

A Five-Step Process for Developing Political Awareness

Once you accept that corporate politics are a given, you can strategize on how to personally navigate them, as well as teach your staff to become more politically savvy. This isn't a one-step process; rather a five-step road map that has helped numerous clients become more aware of the politics waiting to ensnare them and how to proactively avoid them.

Start Your Radar

The first step is getting outside the world of IT and taking an assessment of the people the project will affect. Who are the key stakeholders—the people most affected by the project—and what are their connections, relationships, and previous histories with each other? Beyond the obvious stakeholders, who are the people who believe they should have some say in the project? You need to enlarge your radar screen and not only track but also feel accountable for knowing the people who will be affected by the project.

To do that, you have to become adept at ferreting out information that lives not in the world of facts but in the hidden world of rumor, innuendo, and personal relationships. After all, projects are more about people than technology, and when people come together on projects, they arrive with a whole set of feelings, experiences, goals, and prejudices that you need to understand.

IT professionals may not be accustomed to paying attention to those things. To accomplish their mantra of "on time, on budget, on spec," they actually might consider it noble to ignore the rumor and innuendo that seems to accompany every project they embark on—keep your hands clean and "stick to the facts, ma'am." After all, if you follow logic and make rational decisions based on known facts, isn't that the safest way to an optimal solution?

Unfortunately, the answer is no. Although many IT professionals might like to see the world as a giant problem just waiting to be solved, that approach doesn't account for human feelings, desires, and struggles for power.

To understand the factors that influence our projects, IT professionals need to get to know key stakeholders on a more personal level. You don't need to become close buddies, but you do need to know people well enough to predict their behavior—where they'll form alliances, who their enemies are, who they won't cooperate with, who they're likely to gang up on. Imagine how much more smoothly things would go if you had a better handle on these factors that you might otherwise feel are outside of your control.

Determine Where the Power Bases Are

One of the key things to understand about project stakeholders is the clout they have in the organization. Clout has two dimensions: positional authority, which is where people stand on the corporate ladder, and influence, which is the power they yield outside the organizational chart. People who are highly placed on both dimensions are the obvious movers and shakers to whom project managers need to pay attention. It's possible, though to be influential without high positional authority. There are people who have hidden clout, and it's important to understand who they are, too.

Think back to the television show *M*A*S*H*—Radar is a good example of someone with hidden clout, despite being low in rank. Many administrative assistants are also people who yield a great deal of influence that could help or hinder you, particularly as they might control access to the people you need to get to know.

Understanding how people influence others is essential to the IT professional of the future. The topic is covered further in Chapter 4, on consulting skills.

Sort Your Enemies from Your Allies

Don't fall into the naïve trap of believing that because you and your project sponsor are excited about the project that everyone else is, too. You need to do some stakeholder analysis to figure out who stands to win and to lose from the project—or who perceives themselves as winners or losers. From this analysis, you can predict who your allies and enemies will be, as well as who will ally with you or oppose you.

How people align themselves within a project depends on two key factors. The first is the degree to which they share common interests or WIIFMs on the project (acronym introduced in

Chapter 1). Second is the quality of the relationships they have with one another.

People who share common WIIFMs and who get along well are natural allies. Those who don't get along and who have opposing WIIFMs will be enemies on the project. In between are people who might overlook a bad relationship to ally with those who can help them get their WIIFMs, and people who like each other but can't see eye-to-eye on what they'll get out of the project.

By considering the positions of key players on a project, project managers can develop strategies to move people toward alliance through building strong relationships or promoting shared interests. Where enemies are so strong they can't be moved to less dangerous positions, strategies need to be made to contain potentially damaging behaviors.

Predict the Political Pitfalls, and Chart the Course

From the information you glean in steps 1 to 3, you should be able to predict what might happen from a political perspective on your project. These are the potential political pitfalls you might encounter. What kinds of actions might people take that would be harmful to the project? If someone thinks he stands to lose something and has an influential ally who doesn't like your boss, what might he do to undermine the project?

This process is a kind of risk analysis on a project, but instead of considering the technology risks, you're uncovering the political ones. Once you predict the pitfalls, you can determine what you can do to head off unfortunate events. The concept of clearing the path for change is discussed in Chapter 11.

Stay the Course

The last step is an ongoing one. You have to pay as much attention to your political course as you do to the traditional project plan. If your planned tactics don't work, you need to take corrective action. If a major change happens—like the appointment of a new project sponsor—it would be politically irresponsible to assume the person will have the same priorities as the previous sponsor. And if you find out they don't, you have to restructure your project, not resist the new sponsor's ideas and wish things were different.

For example, I once led an IT team working on a highly visible, multiyear, multimillion-dollar implementation of a major financial system. A couple of years into the project, which was going well, the CFO who'd been the project sponsor was promoted and replaced by another CFO.

I quickly got on the new CFO's calendar, thanks to the rapport I'd established with the CFO's administrator, and invited my boss, the CIO, to the meeting. I started the meeting with a recap of the project and how well it was going. Halfway through my presentation, the CFO pushed back his chair from the desk and stood up, saying, "This is a lot of bull—we're not going to continue with this project."

I confess I was speechless, but the CIO reacted immediately. "What do you mean we're not going to continue?" she said. "We're heading into Year Three of this project and have already spent more than half of the projected budget—we can't just throw that away!"

Not surprisingly, the CFO didn't take kindly to this retort. "Who are you to tell me what I can and can't do?" he said.

In less than five minutes, the relationship between IT and an important project sponsor was destroyed. Even though the CIO knew better, she was so personally invested in her own perspective that she lost sight of what the meeting was really about: bolstering an important relationship.

If the CIO had probed for more information, she would have found out that the CFO had a terrible experience with the system at his previous employer. Right or wrong, it was his prerogative to end the project. Instead of seeing it as wasting money and a lot of hard work, he may have viewed it as not throwing good money after bad. It then becomes IT's job to figure out how to shut down the project expediently and begin focusing on the next steps.

In retrospect, both the CIO and I should have entered the meeting with a better sense of who the CFO was and where he'd come from to better anticipate his reaction. If we weren't caught by surprise, we would have stood a better chance of thinking through our reactions—and not committing political suicide. You can read more about how to navigate these types of tough negotiations in Chapter 5.

Developing Political Skills

Becoming politically savvy doesn't come naturally. IT leaders need to develop skills—both personally and among their staffs, especially among project managers—that will increase political awareness and make the IT organization successful at navigating politically churned-up waters. Here are some of the key skills required.

Creativity

To widen your radar and assess the power bases among a project's key stakeholders (steps 1 through 3), you need to talk with people in the business, and not just at status meetings. This means finding creative ways of putting yourself in places where you'll interact with people socially. Some IT professionals I work with contend that "water cooler conversations" are a waste of time, but it's during these informal encounters that we can build the alliances that enable us to probe for more important information.

But that doesn't mean coming across like a CIA agent. Rather, IT professionals need to encourage informal conversations on topics outside of work—sports, kids, TV shows. These encounters will naturally help them become privy to the information they ultimately want to know, like the history of their business clients' interrelationships.

Grabbing lunch together is a good way to do this. Everyone else in the business except IT has lunch together, and when IT professionals do go out for lunch, it's usually with someone else from IT rather than people important to our projects. But lunch is a great place to meet on neutral ground and probe for information that can be crucial to the project.

The key is to pay attention when people are talking to you or even around you. These informal encounters can be extremely valuable in improving your understanding of your business clients, increasing your empathy, and sharpening your predictions on how they might react to project implications. No longer can we shut out the conversations around us—there's gold in all that noise.

Interpersonal Effectiveness

Because IT focuses so heavily on producing deliverables within constrained schedules and budgets, it's easy to lose focus on the importance of interpersonal relationships. Consider that in sales, the whole focus is on relationships—salespeople operate from the core belief that it's relationships, not features and functions that sell products. Yes, they need to have a decent product to sell, but beyond that, it's the relationships that count.

It's easy to disdain this point of view, but it's an important dimension to understand if you want to steer around political potholes.

Communication

Good communication does not equal providing a robust status report. These reports almost always contain information that means a lot to the IT professionals working on the project—like the features built in to the system and the milestones reached—but has little value to the business clients. Business clients want to know what these accomplishments mean for them and how they contribute to their own goals, as well as what they can expect from IT in the future.

IT professionals need to stop talking about the features and functions of the project and talk more about the business outcomes, and they have to do this outside of written reports. The best communication is achieved face to face—it's hard to develop a relationship through e-mail.

Focus

When leading or managing a project, IT professionals need to define the goals of the project and focus intently on these goals. And this doesn't mean being "on time, on budget, and according to spec." They need to dig deeper than that and define the desired business outcomes of the project and translate those goals into what they as IT professionals need to achieve. It might be a change in behavior among a particular client base or the establishment and acceptance of a new process. This is discussed further in Chapter 7, on gathering business requirements.

Focusing on these goals will help reveal your natural allies, as well as the clients who may feel threatened by the project's implications.

Interests

What's every business client's favorite radio station? WIIFM. By tuning your antenna to that frequency, you're in a much better position to understand the motivation behind people's actions, as well as figure out strategies for encouraging them in the direction you want them to move.

Henry Ford once said, "There is one principle which a man must follow if he wishes to succeed, and that is to understand human nature. I am convinced by my own experience, and by that of others, that if there is any secret of success, it lies in the ability to get another's point of view and see things from his angle as well as from your own."

Flexibility

The business world is not a place of black-and-white, right-or-wrong decisions. What's more, IT can't claim ownership of the right answer, because what might appear to be the right answer from a technology point of view is not always the right answer for the business.

I once worked with an IT organization that identified two different technology solutions for a particular business situation. Solution A had the lowest maintenance costs and was a good fit with the existing IT infrastructure. Solution B required twice as much work for IT in regard to supporting additional technologies and needing to hire more people. The organization presented Solution A as the better alternative.

But look more carefully at this logic—all the reasons for selecting A over B were internally focused and geared toward the convenience of IT. The IT organization was oblivious to the possibility that Solution B might result in three times as much benefit to the business.

It's easy for people to develop tunnel vision about things that they think are important, but success requires adjusting your own point of view. Instead of laying out what you think is a logical argument and expecting everyone to get on board, you need to consider that your preference is not always the right answer. A better approach is presenting all the alternatives with the information required to make the best decision—not presenting the most convenient decision for IT.

Trust

Effective alliances can't be forged unless people trust you. What erodes trust is when IT comes across has having its own agenda rather than striving to understand the client's point of view.

If you don't think trust is important, consider this classic scenario. A project is under way, with IT developing a solution for a client. The project gets derailed, however, because a vendor meets the client at a golf tournament, begins interacting with the client directly—going around the project manager—and steers the client to the vendor's point of view. What happened there? The vendor understood the importance of gaining the client's trust. Instead of wondering why this type of scenario can happen, you can learn from it and begin building your own trusting relationships.

Support

A great way to strengthen relationships is to figure out ways you can be helpful to people, outside the current project's parameters. What keeps your clients awake at night, or what do they dwell on in the shower? If you ever need a favor from someone, it's easier to ask if you've previously helped her out.

Here again, listening is key. Let's say you're having a meeting with a client who has just gotten off the phone and appears distracted. "Sorry," he says, "I'm just really irritated—let's get on with our meeting." What if you encouraged him to tell you what's going on? You might find out he's been back-and-forth with his wife all day over a dispute with their DSL provider. Take it a step further—can you offer to get him in touch with someone you know in telecom that has contacts with the company?

With one simple phone call, you might be able to build a lot of trust and influence with this client that will reap benefits in the future. It has nothing to do with the project, but indirectly, this type of encounter is just as important as meeting a project deadline.

Conflict Management

Things go wrong—it's a truth of any project. That's why it's so important to improve our ability to handle these conflicts and learn to negotiate effectively.

Negotiating means figuring out a way for everyone to feel they've won something. And that means you can't draw a line in the sand—the "I'm right, you're wrong" mentality. By putting yourself in the other person's shoes, you can better work toward your real goal: Getting people from where they are to where you want them to be. And that means figuring out how far you're willing to move to get to that win-win position. Negotiating through conflict is so important that we've dedicated Chapter 5 to that topic.

For example, a newly hired graphics designer approaches IT and asks for a new PC. IT gives him three options, all Windows based. Of course, the designer was thinking more along the lines of a Macintosh—the standard in the graphics design industry but definitely outside the parameters of IT's established architecture. This can turn into a standoff, in which IT imposes its will on the graphics designer. Of course, the graphics department will likely go out and buy what they need from someone else.

A better option would be for IT to allow well-considered exceptions to their architecture. If the graphics department commits to paying for the extra cost of maintaining a Macintosh, IT can permit the variance. Both parties get what they need to be successful. It's when IT draws its lines so deeply that it can't see win-win opportunities that they become ineffective conflict managers.

Conclusion

IT can no longer play the role of bystander in the game of corporate politics. Technology projects today mean change to the status quo, especially as companies use technology to break down traditional silos that exist across their ever-growing and increasingly global businesses. It bears repeating: Where there's technology, there's change, and where there's change, there will be people who perceive themselves as winners and as losers. And that's where political behaviors are born.

It's true that few IT professionals go into this profession with the desire to play politics. But you don't have to become a negative and devious politician; you just need to develop the political savvy to positively influence or even overcome the inevitable politics that technology projects create.

In fact, ignoring the inflammatory nature of IT's work as a change instigator is a perilous practice. Having been awakened to its importance for project success, there is no reason that IT professionals can't learn to navigate the sea of corporate politics.

Top Ten

Tactics for Sharpening Your Political Savvy

10. If you're not influencing your client base, someone else is.
9. It's relationships that sell, not the product itself.
8. Even people way down on the organizational chart can be strong allies—or enemies.
7. Relationships don't exist without trust.
6. The business world isn't always fair—learn enough to predict actions others may take.
5. Don't be a victim or a sideline sitter.
4. Broaden your radar to understand the world beyond IT.

3. Water cooler conversations aren't just a waste of time—they can reveal important hidden truths.

2. It's a lot easier to ask someone for a favor when you've previously helped her with something.

1. Conflict management means figuring out a way for everyone to win.

Specific Actions I Will Take

- ▪
- ▪
- ▪

CHAPTER 9

Marketing IT's Value

Now that you've read this far into the book and have begun to apply the strategies and philosophies my colleagues espouse, you're ready to tackle marketing. This chapter is purposefully near the end of the book, because no one can start marketing an IT organization until the staff's leadership capabilities are developed and it has adopted a service-oriented and consultative mindset, with well-honed skills in change leadership, project management, political savvy, business requirements gathering, and negotiating.

In fact, I believe marketing is the most important of the business disciplines and can be the most fun, as you'll soon discover. The formulation of the IT organization's image as "service provider of choice" is one of the most important factors for a successful IT cultural transformation. By and large our clients don't understand what we do. We need to market internally to have a shot at increasing our credibility, building partnerships, and turning around any negative perceptions. We live in a world in which perception matters, and this is particularly true for internal IT organizations in today's business world. If clients perceive us as mere code changers, network fixers, and PC installers, how will they react when IT tries to move into a more strategic role in the organization?

In other cases, IT damages its own image and reputation by projecting an arrogant air that says, "We know what's best for the business because we're the technical experts." This looks even worse when the organization hasn't taken the time to explain how technology can be a strategic advantage to the business. Meanwhile, IT is competing with external outsourcers, consultants, vendors, and system integrators, which are very adept at getting in front of executive-level decision makers to convince them of the business benefits their companies can provide.

All these reasons explain why IT needs to market internally— to have a shot at increasing its credibility, building partnerships, and turning around any negative perceptions.

It's not about hype and empty promises; it's about creating an awareness of IT's value. It's about changing client perceptions by presenting a clear, consistent message about the value of IT. After all, if you don't market yourself, someone else will, and you might not like the image you end up with.

At this point, you might be asking yourself, "How do I begin to market? My IT staff doesn't even like the 'M' word!" Well, you're not alone. Remember the television ad of the software salesman standing outside the busy executive's door, hounding him with the repeating slogan of, "Soooo, how much software do you wanna buy?" That's what most IT staffers think when they hear the word *marketing*. They wonder, "What does marketing have to do with IT? Why do I need to change my image? I'm already a good developer!" Because marketing is simply not in IT's comfort zone, they revert to what is more natural for them, which is doing their technical job and leaving the job of marketing to someone else, reinforcing the image of, "IT is just a bunch of techies." As you will soon see, it is everybody's job to market in order to obtain the full benefits of your marketing efforts.

Yet many IT organizations have done a very poor job of marketing their capabilities. Even marketing-savvy IT leaders struggle with how to effectively encourage their staffs to adopt a marketing philosophy and consistently promote their ability to be the IT supplier of choice within their organizations.

But I've seen IT organizations that—through formal and informal marketing techniques—are now enjoying increased staff productivity, improved customer loyalty, and a widely held belief in IT's value, not to mention increased project awareness, momentum, and buy-in. When our IT staffs develop credibility and then reinforce that image through their day-to-day interactions with clients, they'll find themselves invited to the table when C-level executives gather to discuss strategic opportunities and initiatives.

In fact, during my 25 years in the IT profession and working with clients throughout the United States and internationally, I've seen IT leaders make great strides in recognizing the strategic advantage of marketing the IT organization to the rest of the company. One client I worked with put together a marketing initiative to key executives that resulted in more business. "More business?" you say; "Why do I need more work to do?" Well, the executives at this particular CIO's company were getting ready to outsource the work to an outside consulting firm. That would have created a whole new set of headaches for the IT department, so the CIO was thrilled that they could keep this in-house.

Another client in the banking industry put together an initiative called "The Key Influencer Program." This IT organization was proactive in researching how it could apply technology to help its company gain a competitive edge in the marketplace and reported their findings to the top brass every six months in a roundtable format. This went a long way in helping to build a positive perception of the IT department.

So, the first step is marketing to the IT organization that marketing is a good thing. This can be done a number of ways, but the most effective is to let your IT staff know how important this is to your success and help them feel accountable for marketing. To elicit positive marketing behaviors from the entire IT team, IT leaders need to tie the marketing mindset to measurements that provide incentive and reward.

I learned about the importance of marketing soon after embarking on my IT career. I had just finished college and was all set to program in Fortran IV. I also knew just enough about marketing to make me dangerous. I was fortunate to land a job with a Fortune 100 computer manufacturing company in Silicon Valley and started doing technical support instead of programming. One of my responsibilities was conducting presentations about our hardware line to potential buyers. Through trial and error, I discovered I would get a lot more applause at the end of my speech if I spiced it up with a little more pizzazz, a lot more benefit statements (WIIFMs), and a bit less on features and functions (this is the critical concept of "What's in It for Me?" defined in Chapter 1). So I started looking for WIIFMs every chance I got, and it became second nature to rattle them off. I guess this got the attention of the vice president, because the next thing I knew, I was plucked from my comfort zone and put in charge of marketing a portfolio of products and services for the IT department to offer our clients. Back to school I went, to bone up on marketing strategies and advertising campaigns. Because at the end of the day, I still wanted that applause.

Over the years, marketing has served me well in all the other aspects of my career—in management, consulting, and training. And through my many years working with IT organizations on their marketing initiatives, I've developed a six-step approach to marketing the value of IT.

Marketing to the IT Department

The best way to begin your marketing efforts is to embed a 24×7 marketing mindset throughout the entire organization, not just in one or two people. Whether our staffs know it or not, marketing has become part of their everyday jobs. Every time they speak with a client or attend a meeting, they create a positive or negative perception in the client's mind for the new system they're implementing, the processes they use to get something done, the organization they work for, and whether they're capable of adding business value or can barely be trusted to keep the e-mail system running.

So the idea of 24×7 marketing is a key mindset we need to pass along to our staffs. They need to become what O&A calls *hallway marketers,* which means they should speak positively about IT every opportunity they get—in the hallway, elevator, parking lot, cafeteria, during and after meetings, and even during social outings.

Even simple changes in phrasing can make a world of difference in how staff members project an image of themselves, their attitude toward their work, and their willingness to help their clients. If a client asks when an application is likely to get delivered, for example, a typical IT professional might say, "We can't deliver that until next Tuesday." Think of how different an impression would be made if they instead responded, "We can deliver that application as early as next Tuesday." Or if a client reports a problem with a recent system upgrade, some IT professionals might say, "I'm not sure where we messed up on that." Wouldn't it be better if they were to say, "We'll look into that and call you by the end of the day."

One client in Canada went as far as publishing a 3×5 mini brochure for the IT department called "Business Value Delivered: The IT Professional's Guide to Delivering Value." Along with the printed vision statement, it also contains the foundation principles of service, change management, and leadership qualities expected of the IT department. Sprinkled throughout are pictures of the IT professionals helping clients.

Another idea is to create a tag line that conveys an identity with which all IT staffers can relate. This will also spill over to your client base as they begin to see a brand recognition they can identify with. One client in northern California took its tag line one step further and created logos on company-colored polo shirts. Over the pocket was an oval with the tag line, "Tech IT Easy." The message was, "We want to make it easy to do business with us." It was a step toward turning around the perception of the department.

At this point, I might add that it will behoove you to include your technical staff in creating these types of creative endeavors. It not only increases their level of buy-in to your marketing efforts, but it can also be fun and a good team-building exercise. You might even be surprised at how creative the analytical thinkers can be. At one point in my career as an IT manager, I had the opportunity to run an Executive Briefing Center for the many customers who bought our company's computers. Our IT area was responsible for assisting the sales people in the technical explanations of our fine hardware. The presentations were held in a beautiful mahogany and marble suite on the ninth floor overlooking Interstate 101.

This new center needed some spiffy color glossy brochures and some brand recognition. After all, we were competing for the time and attention of many busy CEOs, with all the other technology centers deep in the heart of Silicon Valley. Thus, we embarked on a brand-recognition campaign.

The corporate office had already named our center, "The Application Center for Technology," so there wasn't much we could do about changing the name. So a group of us technologists huddled together in a conference room hashing out various ideas for a tag line. We settled on, "The San Jose *A*pplication *C*enter for *T*echnology . . . a great ACT to follow." We were not only more creative than we ever thought we could be, but the whole team also felt an affinity for our new home. And we took it a step further with a silver lightning bolt symbol across the front cover of all collateral materials to signify the new networking connections of TCP/IP over Ethernet (okay, that was a long time ago!).

If it helps your staff, you can think of marketing as educating the clients. One CIO I worked with knew that the word *marketing* wouldn't go over so well, so he substituted the words *Marketing Plan* with *Quality Improvement Plan* (QIP). In essence, he was marketing to the IT staff in terms they could relate to.

This astute CIO also knew that if he handled the rollout of the QIP correctly, he would weed out tedious, low-value tasks and gain more time for satisfying strategic planning work. This was a benefit he stated to the troops during his quality town hall meeting to gain their buy-in.

Build Partnerships

Establishing working relationships with clients can be difficult because it's outside of many IT professionals' comfort zone. But better working relationships build trust and credibility. And trust and credibility are directly tied to people's motivation to work collaboratively. These elements must be in place before we can market our services, and my colleagues, in earlier chapters of the book, have already established the importance of client partnerships.

Both casual and formal interactions can show clients that IT is interested in them and in their needs. For informal interactions, it's absolutely essential to learn how to actively listen to clients, which means acknowledging their issues, listening and responding with empathy, and taking ownership to help them. Active listening is so important that it's covered in depth in Chapter 4, on consulting skills.

Another way that IT leaders can help prepare their IT staffs to take advantage of informal client encounters is to develop and distribute positive press statements or party lines for all new projects, upgrades, rollouts, and implementations that went smoothly, as well as those that didn't go so smoothly. With these tools, the staff can easily draw upon the type of wording that will best establish the new perception you're trying to create. These press statements should be clear, concise, and client-focused, not long, elaborate PowerPoint presentations. Remember that marketing is a 24×7 mindset, and you will want to do hallway marketing at every casual client encounter.

There are also more formal ways to strengthen client relationships, like planning visits to their workplace. At one large manufacturer, the IT leader encourages members of his team to schedule regular visits to the company's 18 plants to make sure that all systems are functioning smoothly and to ward off potential problems. The staff spends time talking to customers to ferret out any issues—even if they haven't called the help desk to fix them.

Another director of IT that I worked with established the MBWA Program. Using Tom Peters's Management by Walking Around concept, he conducts scheduled and unscheduled visits to his clients on a routine basis to get to know them better and build relationships. At one such visit, the client went to retrieve some information off the mainframe, and the IT director watched in horror as it took 30 seconds to fill the screen. His client casually mentioned that this was typical. With one phone call, the IT director was able to get a much better response time for his client. He told me, "I would never have known about this issue if I hadn't been doing a little MBWA."

Differentiate Yourself

To differentiate the IT organization effectively, you first must understand what matters most to your client. Clients have different business drivers and different intrinsic motivators—in other words, different reasons for making the decisions they make.

For example, take a look at automobile advertisements on television. Have you ever noticed that different ads appeal to different motivations or market segments? If you watch an ad for a

Cadillac, you'll notice they're appealing to the status and image mindset of the buyer. For Volvo, the campaign is around safety and security. For the Saturn, the value being emphasized is economy and getting the best bang for your buck. These advertisements are soliciting to the core values, or intrinsic motivators, of the consumer. The same concept applies to marketing in IT. You will want to appeal to the core values or intrinsic motivators of your client, as well as the business motivators of your client. Business motivators, or benefits, include things like increasing market share, decreasing costs, improving efficiencies, and increasing profits.

I often see IT leaders make the mistake of enthusiastically embarking on a marketing effort that focuses on all the great technology the organization has implemented or plans to implement. Even IT organizations that have made great strides as marketers still talk too much about the features of their systems and services without focusing on how those features benefit clients and the business.

Making technology your marketing focus is like trying to climb a ladder without stepping on all the rungs. You're reaching too far, too soon, and by skipping all those steps in between, you're putting yourself in an unnecessarily precarious situation, with no guarantee you'll make it all the way to the top.

For example, say you've implemented a new firewall or just completed a system upgrade. You can't expect clients to get all excited about new security features or faster speeds and feeds. They want to know what the business benefit is. How does the firewall improve their work lives? Does the upgrade mean reports will get into their hands faster? How can they make better business decisions just because IT has implemented the next version of software? The answers to these questions must be clearly articulated by IT, and yet much of the time, we don't do that.

It's the difference between looking through a pure technology lens and trying to see things from the perspective of the client. I was working with a client in Oregon who told me the following story: She was visiting a client to determine business requirements when the client said to her, "You IT people are like used car salesmen. All you talk about is technology." She said she learned a valuable lesson that day—always talk in terms the client understands.

That's why IT leaders need to learn how to package their organization's day-to-day communications, business cases, and marketing plans in terms of business outcomes and client WIIFMs. We need to focus our efforts on promoting the business problem-solving capabilities of IT. Remember the old sales adage, "People don't buy drill bits because they want a drill bit. People buy drill bits because they want a hole."

Establish Credibility

Peter F. Drucker argued, "Business has only two functions—marketing and innovation." I propose a corollary that in marketing, "presentation and perception are everything."

We already discussed the importance of hallway marketing and creating a positive impression of the IT department 24×7. But it's not easy to know how others perceive us. We think we're smart, witty, and reasonable, while others perceive us as sarcastic, self-serving, and helplessly removed from reality. One way to be sure you know how IT is perceived is to conduct a survey. A simple questionnaire with easy Yes and No checkboxes will give you the information you need. Ask your clients to rate your staff on some of the following:

- Are we professional and courteous?
- Do we provide quick response time?
- Do we understand your business needs?
- Do we provide alternatives to problems?

What you want to do is assess the level of trust your clients have in you and your team, and uncover any expectations you weren't aware of so you can address any problems with a concrete marketing plan.

I saw this most successfully achieved when I was in a consulting role for O&A back in 1999. One of the most successful CIOs I know, and also one of my favorites for creative thinking outside the box, hired O&A to conduct a survey of key agency heads in the county in which he was employed. He had heard some rumblings that the IT department wasn't perceived as positively as it could have been. In fact, since he was recently hired by the county as the new CIO, there was even more skepticism about what changes he might impose. Obviously, there was a lot of mistrust between IT and the client base.

As a result of the survey, a marketing plan was put in place to address each agency director's key concerns about the IT department. This CIO literally went about changing the perception one by one through a formal plan. Fast-forward five years, and I'll tell you that this CIO was able to go from a rating of "No Trust" from most agencies to being honored as one of the top 100 CIOs in the country by *Computerworld* magazine. Ironically enough, it was one of the toughest agency directors that nominated him for this prestigious award.

Create Product and Service Awareness

Now that you've built strong relationships, increased your credibility through positive press statements and hallway marketing, demonstrated that you understand client needs and WIIFMs, you are finally ready to market your products and services.

In my work with clients, I often hear, "I'm not sure what IT even does." And worse yet, I hear from IT employees, "I don't even know what other IT departments do." So before you can market the added value you bring to the business, you must let business clients—and each other—know what you already offer.

To do this, some IT organizations stage open houses, inviting directors and managers and other key staff to educate them on the services that IT provides and on how to better communicate their technology needs and issues. They might reinforce the message with pamphlets documenting IT's services and key phone numbers, as well as brochures giving customers tips on how to solve some of the most common IT problems.

One client I worked with was about to move the call center from one location to a brand new building. The IT organization took this opportunity to market the event as a Grand Re-Opening with a new tag line, new furniture, and a new catchy help desk phone number of IT-911. It sent out invitations to directors and managers in the businesses and asked them to bring key staff. A tour of the new facility followed a brief presentation on how the new call center would operate. The organization also handed out a pamphlet, documenting its services and how best to get in touch with the help desk, as well as a brochure providing tips on the Top Ten Frequently Asked Questions at the Help Desk. Refreshments were served, and trinkets were handed out with the call center's name and new phone number on them.

Another IT organization held a weeklong IT Spirit Week in its headquarters, presenting demos and tutorials, as well as a simple lunch for clients who stopped by to learn more about IT and its services. The week culminated with an ice cream social and a drawing for a few flat-screen monitors.

One of my favorites is the client who revamped the Brown Bag Lunchtime Seminar as The Gold Bag Executive Luncheon. Once a quarter, this IT department hosts a catered lunch for their C-level executives in the dining room. They give a presentation on the latest and greatest technology that the execs have been reading about in in-flight airline magazines and discuss how this technology may or may not fit the corporate architecture. It sounds like it's a bit on the techie side, but it actually helps the executives get a handle on what's possible in their company from a strategic advantage perspective.

In another case, I know a savvy IT director in Los Angeles who planned a way to showcase her new team after a recent merger between two companies and subsequently two IT departments. She invited Midwest clients who weren't familiar with the new IT department to a tour of the data center, followed by tickets to a Dodgers game. It was a big hit and helped build morale during the merger and forge new relationships, at the same time introducing the new IT department.

Lastly, I'd like to tell the story about one of the first pieces of marketing collateral I ever created. It was a quick guide to the services our IT organization offered outside our company. Our client base was the sales organization that would be selling our technical services to our outside customers. We came up with what we thought was a pretty catchy guidebook, with a working title of, "Selling IT Services." Before we put it into print, however, we brought it to several client focus groups that told us it was boring and not compelling enough. After much deliberation, we revamped it to, "The EASY Way to Sell IT Services," and it was a big hit.

This leads me to an important part of marketing, and that is the use of what I like to call *magic words*. Magic words are special words that capture the attention of customers, like *easy, new, announcing, free,* and *how to.* It's important to note, however, that not only must your collateral fit the needs of the client, it also must avoid being too glitzy if IT is perceived as a high-overhead organization. Think it through—are color handouts necessary when black-and-white will do? If you're too professional looking in your marketing materials, you may fall prey to criticism of spending too much on marketing.

Develop a Formal Plan

You might be thinking that the last thing IT needs is yet another plan. But savvy IT leaders ensure that marketing plans are developed and executed at multiple levels of the organization, such as the executive level, business unit level, and team level.

Just like any project plan, there are many factors to consider when rolling out a marketing plan. A few of these include:

- The overall goal of the marketing plan—what you hope to accomplish with it and ways to evaluate its success. For example, do you want to market your image and credibility or go right to marketing value-add? How will you know you've been successful?
- Risks and assumptions, as well as factors to consider that might hinder the marketing process, such as corporate culture and reorganization timing.
- Types of awareness programs and relationship-building strategies you can realistically roll out, given budget and staff restrictions.
- Tag lines and themes to garner brand recognition.
- Factors that might affect successful marketing, such as past history or perceptions by the clients.

After reviewing these considerations, put your conclusions in writing so that you have a well-thought-out marketing strategy or even a checklist that the entire team can get behind. Anticipate any questions or reactions you might get and have a response plan. Here's where your press statements come in.

Determining Success

So, how do you know when you've succeeded with your marketing efforts? What are the indicators of a good marketing plan? Number one is defining up front what will determine success, not waiting until the end. You need to know before you begin what you want to happen as a result of your efforts.

Other indicators include:

- Your clients requesting that IT be more involved in their business, such as inviting you to business planning and strategy meetings or having you review and influence their technology decisions
- Having your budget requests met without having to constantly justify your existence and contributions
- Your current clients referring others to you, or that you can imagine your clients saying, "Hey, IT really helped us out," versus "Oh, those IT people!"
- Requests for your assistance becoming more focused and more in line with the products and services you actually provide
- Unsolicited positive feedback both formal and informal from your clients and senior management
- Morale across IT is high
- IT being included in merger and acquisition negotiations and due diligence
- IT being included in meetings and sales processes with big C-level clients

A word to the wise: There's no guarantee that everyone will automatically applaud the services you're marketing. After all, clients have a past history with IT and perhaps some preconceived notions of what IT people are all about. To be successful in executing your marketing efforts, you need to anticipate and plan for the factors that can derail them. Solid marketing plans acknowledge and address both positive and negative impacts up front, with an appropriate press statement to minimize resistance.

For example, imagine you were marketing your new mission statement. What about the client group that's constantly asking you to provide wireless services, which is not part of your mission? You can anticipate that they'll be less than thrilled with your message, unless you plan a response to any questions they have about their wireless needs.

Take into consideration other negative impact factors, such as:

- Past history or perceptions that clients have had with the marketing effort
- External or internal competition
- Economic factors such as budgets
- Corporate culture factors such as politics or impending reorganizations
- Current projects or systems that aren't being well received
- Technical constraints, such as standards, security, and documentation

Conclusion

For many IT professionals, it requires a dramatic change of mindset to start promoting the work they do. But it's worth it, because it's becoming a crucial element of the IT leader's job to show the business that the IT organization is capable of being the strategic business partner of choice.

We can begin by understanding how our organizations are perceived—rightly or wrongly—and then crafting a plan for gaining control over how we want to be understood. This can be accomplished by bridging gaps of miscommunication with clients; understanding their needs and strategic objectives and then showing them the IT organization is capable of meeting those needs. When business clients develop a new awareness of IT's true value, the IT organization's own marketing message can be heard above the very aggressive campaigns launched by internal IT's competitors—external vendors and service providers.

When you combine a marketing mindset focusing on the client, and add in some positive hallway marketing, you'll get a successful, well positioned, marketing-savvy IT organization whose value is understood enterprise wide.

Top Ten

Approaches for Marketing IT's Value

10. Conduct internal market research to better understand client needs.
9. Develop a mission statement, clear goals, and objectives that define who you are.
8. Design a tag line that the whole team can endorse.
7. Create a promotional strategy that is long term and high impact.
6. Develop long-term client relationships.
5. Design positive press statements for use in hallway marketing.
4. Forge stronger partnerships with your most difficult clients.
3. Adopt a frame of mind that constantly asks, "Who is my client?" and "What services can I offer that client?"
2. Project a team image by changing *I* to *We*.
1. Speak in terms of benefits rather than features.

Specific Actions I Will Take

-
-
-

CHAPTER 10

Managing the Vendor Relationship

In the IT profession, it's practically guaranteed that you will work with a service provider—if you don't already. But it's almost equally guaranteed that you've never been taught how to do this, or trained your staff on vendor relationship management skills; in fact, it may not have even occurred to you that managing the service provider relationship requires skills, disciplines, processes, and knowledge that you may not have.

The fact is, managing a service provider—be it an outsourcer, software-as-a-service provider, or cloud vendor—goes way, way beyond developing a good contract. You're managing a relationship, and the contract happens to just be a formal document structuring the relationship.

It is also much more complex than buying products from a vendor. When you're managing service providers who work side by side with your own staff—and provide direct service to clients and customers—there are complexities and problems that are not as apparent when purchasing a product.

Managing a service provider is also decidedly very different from managing a staff of employees. In fact, these two disciplines—managing relationships versus employees—are as different as night and day. With employees, you're sharing a common objective with the staff, which is to grow company revenue and meet business objectives and goals.

With the service provider's staff, you're on two different missions, as they're focused on maximizing their employer's value. They are not there to promote you, and their entire reward system is based on making money off you. Their focus is on locking you, the customer, into a long-term technology and financial commitment and making sure those revenues are delivered every year at a high margin. They are looking for leverage in the relationship, however they can get it, and they want to maximize your dependency on their products and services.

The perils of doing this wrong range from lost opportunity to lost revenue to lost reputation. Get it right, on the other hand, and you'll reap the true benefits available from the provider. Indeed, the ability to effectively manage the providers of services can be a competitive advantage.

Both Sides of the Coin

Take it from me—since starting my career in the 1970s, I've seen both sides of the coin: fruitful and productive service provider relationships, as well as the dysfunctional and even deceitful. I've worked in many industries—from insurance to financial services to energy—at large, highly regulated organizations, as well as fast-growth start-ups. I've also led major initiatives, from corporate-wide process improvement efforts, to developing corporate strategic plans.

Very early in my career, I learned firsthand the value you can get from a strong service provider relationship. I was working for a 150-person start-up company, whose goal was to create a fully online automated property and casualty insurance company in nine months' time. We worked hand in hand with IBM, using the newest IBM hardware and software and with their top people onsite on a daily basis. We achieved our goal, and they got something out of it, too, as we were in the forefront of using what was then one of their cutting-edge products, and they could transfer that knowledge to other clients.

I wasn't prepared, then, for a later experience I had while working with a consulting firm. The existing contract with a provider for applications development work unintentionally favored the vendor. The established performance metrics in the open-ended contract were geared around the number of lines of Cobol code they produced. Well, as you can imagine, this is a completely useless metric. If you take four lines of code to do something you could accomplish in one, you can claim a 400 percent increase in productivity.

Also, our corporate cultures were vastly different. My staff was a down-to-earth, blue-collar group, while these guys were smooth, highly articulate, and well-dressed. Their attitude seemed to be that they were hired because we were incompetent. It didn't take long before the finger-pointing began. Any problem that came up, they'd attribute it to someone on my staff, and next thing I knew, they were trying to make an end run around me and align people in my company against me. "If Ken says anything you disagree with, just let us know, and we'll go straight to his boss," they'd say. Finally, after more of these kinds of tactics, the president of the firm had enough. They were let go and told to never come back.

Less dramatic but still instructive was the time my company contracted with a large provider for our telecommunications infrastructure. We neglected to define an escalation process in the contract, so when all of New England lost service for two solid days, and we weren't getting a response from the provider, I ended up having to call the chairman to get a response. You can imagine I learned from that, and have inserted an escalation clause ever since.

With that range of experience, I feel so strongly that managing the service provider relationship is not something you can just throw your staff into without training them in the relevant skills, knowledge, and disciplines. And with more companies than ever using service providers for everything from applications hosting, to business process outsourcing, the stakes have gotten way too high to continue with a haphazard, undisciplined approach.

Preparing for a New Role

IT certainly has years of experience with outsourcing, and we're probably better at it than many other areas of the company. But there are so many ways of doing it wrong. We're outsourcing the wrong things; failing to analyze our business processes before outsourcing them; creating the wrong metrics or failing to measure at all; focusing on rates versus total cost; paying more attention to the contract than the relationship. One client told me recently that he was spending a good third of his time arguing with his service provider about what was in or out of the contract—a total waste of time.

We're failing to inform vendors of our dissatisfaction before it's too late, taking no action to bridge differing corporate cultures, and significantly underestimating the staffing it takes to manage the relationship. You can't just tell a vendor to do something; you have to monitor and manage it, and that takes time and energy.

There are obvious signs that emerge when your vendor management disciplines are not up to par. These range from arguing, complaints, disagreement over small changes, friction between your own staff and the outside organization. Over time, the pain points grow, and organizations risk their reputation by missing deadlines and incurring higher-than-expected costs, while receiving lower-than-expected quality and lower staff morale.

We can no longer overlook that outsourcing requires additional work; indeed, the very role of the IT leader is inevitably shifting from one of selecting and managing employees, to selecting and managing vendor partnerships. Some of the new roles that IT leaders need to be prepared for include working directly with the provider, leading change management efforts, integrating vendor processes with the company's, and monitoring external process metrics.

Done well, these behaviors and skills can lead to a strong relationship with the service provider, enabling you to accomplish so much more than just lowering the costs of your IT operations. You can maximize your IT assets, more easily meet your business objectives, encourage innovation for improved processes and products, and even ensure you've got a partner to help in times of trouble or survival.

A good example comes from a client that worked to forge a good relationship with his service provider. During the recent downturn, this client went to the vendor and confided that he needed to make some budget cuts, and he asked for help. A week later, the vendor offered to reduce its rates by 7 percent for the following year. This type of win-win action would simply not have happened without a good relationship to begin with.

Getting to this level means getting off on the right foot with the service provider and staying there. This requires engaging in new disciplines and processes even before you've selected the outsourcing vendor. In fact, there are actually seven different phases that determine relationship quality (see Figure 10.1):

1. Process evaluation
2. Deciding what should be insourced and what should be outsourced
3. Vendor selection
4. Contract development and negotiations
5. Implementation of the working relationship
6. Management of the relationship
7. Evaluation of the results

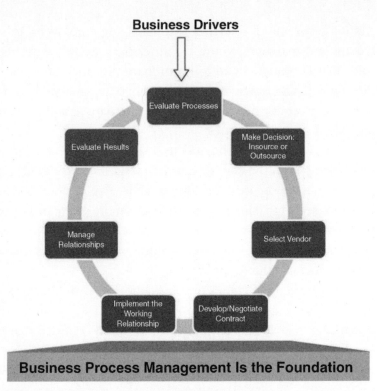

FIGURE 10.1 Managing Vendor Partnerships Model

Getting a Fresh Start

Let's go through each of these phases in detail. But before we get into that, I first want to address three preliminary points that are essential to explore before you even embark on improving your vendor relationships.

1. *Know why you're outsourcing.* There are three primary reasons why companies look outside the internal IT organization for technology services: cost control, the desire to focus on core competencies, and supply-demand fluctuation. Very often, however, when I ask clients why they're outsourcing, they don't know what the goals are. And even when they do

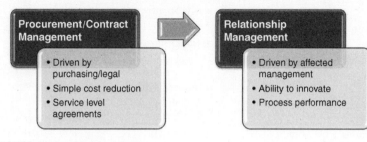

FIGURE 10.2 Mindset Change

know, they're not using metrics that tell them whether they're meeting those goals. The vast majority of people I encounter say they're outsourcing to control costs, and yet only about half use cost as a metric. So, it's important to understand why you're outsourcing, in the context of the corporate strategy.

2. *Make a mindset change.* To forge a good vendor relationship, you need to shift your mindset from contract management to relationship management, or from the left to the right in Figure 10.2.

3. *Decide on the type of partnership you want.* Not all service provider relationships are the same, and before embarking on one, you need to determine which partnership will best help you achieve your goals.

There are three main types of partnerships: provider, collaborator, and alliance (see Figure 10.3). *Provider* is the most basic, hands-off type of relationship, sometimes referred to in the industry as, "lift and shift." In provider relationships, companies are mainly looking to the vendor to take over mundane or back office processes to reduce costs through labor arbitrage. *Collaborator* is a more complex and value-driven relationship, in which companies are looking for process improvements from the vendor. The third type, *Alliance,* involves the company and vendor forming a partnership through which they jointly create and market

	Provider	Collaborator	Alliance
Company	Contracts for specific levels, volumes, and quality of service	Open with information and willing to share ideas with the vendor to achieve a mutually beneficial set of goals	The company and vendor: • Enter into a complex market relationship in which they share all risks and rewards of the undertaking • Develop a joint marketing approach • Plan the business together • Share investments and returns
Vendor	Commits to providing a bundle of products and services	Provides ideas and innovations for improvements in the performance of the business process it manages and for the customer operation as a whole	

FIGURE 10.3 Three Types of Vendor Partnerships

software or other innovations and share in any profits and royalties.

Based on my own observations, about 77 percent of the contracts and relationships I encounter fall into the provider category, about 20 percent are collaborator, and the remaining 3 percent are alliance. In truth, because the collaborator relationship provides so much more value to the organization, most execs would like to see that percentage boosted to about 50 percent. It's the difference between hiring a provider to answer the phones on your help desk and contracting with the vendor to reduce problem resolution times.

But the important thing is to know which partnership you want to be in—what value you're trying to get from the relationship—because it affects everything else you do, including which provider you choose, the contents of the contract, the performance metrics and incentives you use, and the governance structure you build.

For example, you can't expect to get collaborator-level value from the partnership when the contract is designed for a provider relationship. On the flip side, I had a client tell me she was trying to work out contract terms at a collaborator level, and the vendor kept pulling back to provider-type terms; I told her, it's probably not the right choice of vendor—some aren't set up to be collaborators.

Seven Phases of Managing Vendor Partnerships

Now we're ready to discuss the seven different phases that determine relationship quality. After all, a good vendor relationship doesn't start with the contract; it begins even before you've selected the outsourcing vendor.

Phase 1: Process Evaluation

A close look at most business processes today will reveal cross-departmental processes that are fragmented, unmeasured, unmanaged, and disconnected. There is no use outsourcing such a mess—that's where the phrase "your mess for less" comes from! You're just asking the vendor to take over where you left off, with a suboptimal and possibly detrimental, process. Even if the vendor claims to make improvements, you'll have no baseline from which to determine that improvement.

To see the benefits of outsourcing, you need a true understanding of your processes, including their outputs and end-to-end costs. You then need to create meaningful and balanced performance metrics to measure process improvement and prevent dysfunctional behavior. The goal is to establish a shared understanding with the vendor about performance and management expectations and to create a mutual understanding about process improvement opportunities.

I could dedicate an entire chapter to doing just this! But a good start is to understand two things: What makes a good metric, and how do you choose a set of metrics that will help you achieve your desired results.

Basically, good metrics can be summarized as having the following characteristics:

- Accuracy: Reliably expresses what is being measured
- Objectivity: Not subject to dispute
- Ease: Inexpensive and convenient to compute
- Timeliness: Data sources are available
- Comprehensibility: Can be readily communicated and understood
- Harmlessness: Does not induce dysfunctional behaviors
- Holistic: Avoids suboptimization
- Meaningful: Ties back to the business and the value it brings to service delivery

To arrive at what is most meaningful for a given process, it's best to look at things from a client point of view. Here's a non-IT example. Say you're a utility, and you've chosen these four metrics: Cost per customer, elapsed time, percent of uncollectibles, and customer satisfaction. Then, let's say you decide to outsource your customer call center, and you define your vendor performance metrics based on driving down the cost per call.

But does this make sense? Think again. A common customer call involves complaining about a bill that is unusually high despite electricity use being the same as the month before. If the outsourcer is being rewarded based on cost per call, he'll be motivated to quickly end the call by dispatching a meter reader to ascertain whether the reading was correct or not. But what effect will this have on the holistic cost of doing business, let alone customer satisfaction?

Now, what if cost per customer and customer satisfaction were chosen as the performance metrics? In this case, when the customer calls, the outsourcer would stay on the phone, tell them how to read the meter, and provide them with instant feedback. Not only does this improve customer satisfaction, but it also reduces costs, since taking that extra few minutes on the phone is a lot cheaper than sending out an employee to read a meter. By building in the right incentives and rewards, you can go beyond reducing costs within the function, to improving the process as a whole.

The same principles can be applied to the help desk. One client I worked with told me their chosen metric for optimizing the help desk was to measure how quickly they could get something off the desk's hands and into another department for resolution. But a better metric could be obtained by looking at things from the client's point of view. Clients get frustrated when they need to make a lot of calls to the help desk, so really, it should have been focused on reducing the volume of incoming calls. And clients don't care how quickly you get work off the help desk; they just want the problem fixed as quickly as possible.

Success is also geared around looking at processes from end to end, not in a siloed, disconnected way. For example, I'm a big believer in grouping application development under the same process owner as application maintenance. If you're being rewarded for low application development costs and are unconcerned with maintenance—where the costs are traditionally highest over the lifetime of the application—you won't be developing with maintenance in mind. By bringing the two under one process owner and one reward system, the people doing development are going to think very hard about the ease of maintaining the systems they create.

Here's another example of metrics gone wrong: A company I knew drove down its travel costs by limiting travel in favor of webcasting and videoconferencing. Meanwhile, IT costs were going up. So while the travel unit was rewarded, IT was slammed for rising costs, even though, in the end, this was the best solution for the company.

Overall, the siloed mentality creates a situation in which everyone is working to optimize his piece of the puzzle as opposed to looking at the whole picture. So when you bring in a vendor to manage the process, you want to be sure you incent her in a way that will improve the process and not just handle an individual function.

Phase 2: Determine What Should Be Insourced and What Should Be Outsourced

Once you have a handle on your processes, you can more objectively evaluate which are most beneficial to be outsourced. There are varying philosophies around how to make this decision, and clearly—as seen by the number of companies that reverse their decision to outsource and bring the work back in-house—many ways to get this wrong, as well. Regardless, the decision is all the more clear when you analyze your business processes and determine which are in most need of optimization and whether your internal IT organization is up to the task or needs the help of an expert.

One consideration that many companies use when deciding what to outsource is to identify which processes are core to the company's competitive strategy and which are noncore. However, I think this is a very subjective approach. If you've spent your entire career in IT working on a particular area, the chances are high that you'll consider that to be core.

An example from my own experience is when I worked at a large insurance company, where one of our core business areas was an investment management function. But even though we were very large and fast-growing, we couldn't seem to hire the best investment managers compared to the very largest investment management companies. Eventually, we outsourced the function, despite its being a core process, and we focused on using our marketing sales force to beat the competition.

188

These types of examples are why I prefer to advise companies to focus on areas in which they've developed the most specialized skills and to keep that work in-house, with particular attention to the industry in which they're operating. For example, when I was in financial services, we outsourced all of our telecommunications work; however, at the utility, communication was much more intensive, with field staff traveling throughout the state and remote service centers outside of the main headquarters. In that case, we outsourced some of our telecommunications work and retained some in-house.

Whatever approach you take, don't make the decision to outsource lightly. Once you outsource something, it's very difficult to bring it back in-house. I know of companies that realized after a few years that outsourcing a particular process was a terrible mistake and that it can take years to unwind that decision and reestablish the process in-house.

Phase 3: Vendor Selection

In the early days of outsourcing, it was common to choose vendors solely on the basis of cost—who responded with the lowest price point. Today, we've moved well beyond that simplistic viewpoint, and most companies realize that there are many more elements to consider. At the same time, I still see companies stepping on some common hidden minefields and missing out on best practices that can easily be incorporated into the selection process.

One hidden obstacle that I encounter on a regular basis is companies overlooking the vendor's internal culture and how well it meshes with their own. When I say culture, I'm not just talking about the differences among global and regional cultures, although that's obviously a big factor. But there are other, more subtle and easily missed corporate cultural differences that can really trip you up if you don't detect them, work to bridge the gap, or decide that the divide is too big to overcome.

Some important cultural differences to be aware of include:

- Time orientation: Punctual versus ill-defined
- Organizational structure: Hierarchical versus collaborative
- Decision making: Top down versus distributed
- Rate of change: Rapid versus slow
- Age of workforce: Older versus younger

While you'll never find a company that's just like yours, you can avoid frustration by minimizing the cultural gaps and knowing beforehand where the differences will be greatest. The ideal situation is to analyze cultural differences before you even select the outsourcing vendor; for companies that are already working with a vendor, however, there are many ways to harmonize the differences, whether through training, team-building exercises, and working to understand the expectations of the vendor. The key is to measure the gap and then to bridge it with communications and greater levels of understanding.

Another important aspect of vendor selection is researching whether the vendor has previous experience with the work you want them to do and whether it has worked in an environment that's similar to your own. For example, if you're a global company, you don't want to hire someone whose biggest client had just a few thousand employees.

Due diligence is also essential. Does the vendor have standardized processes, economies of scale, financial stability? One client told me her standard practice was to look closely at the vendor's last two financial quarters. You should also research the lawsuits brought against the vendor by previous clients. I remember years ago finding out, accidentally, that half the clients of a vendor I was considering had filed lawsuits. While these are not always publicized, it's easy to investigate these days through Internet searches.

Once you've developed a short list of potential vendors, you should share with them some of your plans, strategies, business objectives, and process improvement goals. At one company I worked for, we spent the better part of a day presenting our future IT strategy to 20 potential vendors. At the end of the presentation, we asked them to come back and give us their plan on how they could help us implement that strategy. By letting them know exactly what we were trying to accomplish, we got a feel for their style of work.

Once you get down to the actual selection time, be sure to include the key departments involved with the process or function you plan to outsource. These process owners need to feel engaged and involved in the outsourcing decision, and they need to understand what you're trying to accomplish. Other people who should be at the table include representatives from the procurement, financial, and legal aspects of the business. In fact, some companies are co-locating procurement specialists where the outsourcing activity is most concentrated, to get their input into areas of improvement. I'm also increasingly seeing representatives from the cyber-security team at the table.

On the vendor side, be sure to meet with the actual people with whom you'll be interfacing on a regular basis. Don't just talk to the sales people working on the deal, because they're prone to make promises they have no idea how to keep.

The overall point is to make this a team effort and get process owners involved early on. You don't want to do all the legwork and bring in these key players after you've made the selection.

Phase 4: Contract Development and Negotiations

The team mentality needs to be carried over into the contract development and negotiations phase. In many companies, outsourcing contracts are signed by purchasing, legal, and senior executives and then "thrown over the wall" to the managers who will be involved with the vendor day-to-day.

As with vendor selection, operational staff and process owners should be involved early on, not after the contract is signed. This level of employee can provide valuable input to creating true ways of measuring performance that are conducive to a partnership.

In the Managing Vendor Partnerships workshops I've conducted across the country, I've seen people who were trying to manage the relationship who had never seen the contract! How can they possibly be expected to manage the vendor when they don't even know what metrics were established? Simply put, the people involved with negotiating the contract need to be the ones who have to live with the results. By being involved, they will also be able to ramp up more quickly once the engagement begins, because they were engaged and involved from the beginning. Ultimately, there's less chance of things falling through the cracks.

During contract negotiations, it's important to keep the competitive level high and provide plenty of incentives for the vendor to give you a good deal. For example, this is an optimal time to outline for the vendor the potential for future business at your company, if performance levels are met. You should also keep two or more companies in the bidding. Too often, people zero in on one company, and this results in vendor complacency. This is also true when it's time to renew the contract. I remember at one company I worked with, we had a large contract with a provider for all our call and service centers in the state. When it was time to re-up the contract, we put it out for bid, and another provider came in at 10 percent less, to which our vendor responded with a 13 percent cut in price.

Another way to keep negotiations competitive is to use different providers for closely knit functions or processes. For example, I've seen cases in which AT&T handled the international side of telecom for a business, and MCI the domestic side. Each knew they could pick up business from the other if they provided great service, and that kept them operating competitively. If a vendor thinks it has a lock on your business, it will grow complacent about providing great service.

Here are three key items to consider building into any contract you sign:

1. *Clearly outlined roles for the vendor, as well as your staff.* This will help you avoid the all too common situation of internal staff continuing to do work that the vendor is being paid to do. This often happens because of confusion over contracted responsibilities or because people are simply reluctant to let their roles go.
2. *Flexibility to renegotiate under certain conditions.* If the vendor gains new capabilities or begins to offer new cost structures, you want to take advantage of that. I recently saw a client successfully renegotiate its contract after the vendor completed an acquisition so they could use the capabilities of the acquired company. Conditions for renegotiation can include changes in functional requirements, technology, cost structure, and vendor capabilities.
3. *Control over the workforce.* An advantage of using a service provider versus hiring employees is that you can build into the contract the right to remove employees who are unsuitable to your environment. I'm also increasingly seeing companies build in penalties for exceeding a defined level of turnover. Something vendors do for their own advantage is have staff learn from you and then apply those newly developed skills to another client. One of my clients told me they'd had 200 percent turnover over a two-year period! You can waste a lot of time constantly retraining the vendor's staff.

Throughout the process, remember that contract negotiations should not be all about the contract. This is also a good time to build trust and develop the foundation for future team-work by sharing stories and engaging in informal conversation. Sometimes we can get caught up in contract terms and forget that it's equally important to work together as a team.

Phase 5: Implementation of the Working Relationship

So you've selected the vendor and negotiated the contract, hopefully with the goal of establishing a collaborative partnership with the vendor. Now it's time for the rubber to meet the road, and for this to happen, you need to create an atmosphere at your company that encourages collaboration. This means ensuring lots of communication between IT, the process owners, all the internal clients affected by the change and the supplier itself.

Here are some tips for creating an environment that is conducive to collaboration:

- *Communicate with the vendor about company goals, as well as process strategies.* Something I hear in my workshops and consulting work is that companies are not being open and transparent enough with vendors on their priorities and objectives—that, purposely or not, they're prone to keeping the vendor in the dark.

  To encourage service providers to support the strategy of the business, you need to intentionally educate them on business drivers and long- and short-term strategies.

- *Create mechanisms for the supplier to interface directly with internal clients.* This may seem dangerous, as we've all heard of instances when vendors try to cozy up to business clients to leverage the relationship and perhaps sell them on things they don't want. But the fact is, it's to your advantage for vendors to hear directly from your clients—the good, the bad, and the ugly—as long as you facilitate these communications and ultimately maintain control over the internal client relationship.

Some of my clients say they host brown-bag lunches for the vendor and internal clients to encourage these conversations. Any kind of face-to-face meetings, including presentations and workshops, with IT staff, vendor, and internal clients in attendance can go a long way toward getting everyone on the same page.

- *Incent the vendor by promoting them*. Everyone likes a win-win arrangement, and vendors are no different. To maintain a positive relationship, some companies have begun sponsoring annual vendor recognition awards. They establish certain criteria, and if the vendor gets a high score, they get some type of reward, as well as the ability to brag about being chosen as one of your top vendors. It can be a motivator for them to work harder for that kind of recognition.

- *Gain the commitment of the internal staff*. One of the most difficult things to accomplish when outsourcing is getting acceptance and commitment from the remaining staff. Too often, clients and internal IT are unclear on the expectations that have been established and what roles have been assigned to the staff and the vendor. They are also uncertain as to why the particular work has been outsourced, why this particular vendor has been chosen, what the expectations are and what their role is.

For people whose jobs are changing, it's a very stressful time. The antidote is to spend time educating everyone involved on the changes taking place, from departmental meetings, to one-on-one coaching. This requires well-honed change management skills and disciplines, which we cover thoroughly in the next chapter.

It's very important during a stress-filled time like an outsourcing transition to be unified in your messaging about the changes taking place. If the leaders of the transition are conveying different messages to different groups, people are going to get even more confused, fearful, and resistant. You have to overcome what could be a chaotic time and prepare a formal change management strategy.

To gain trust, it's also important not to pull punches. Some companies incorrectly think they can create a sense of calm by reassuring people that there will be no change in the levels of service they're used to. In the short term, this is most likely not true. Anytime you turn a function over to an outside group, there will likely be a temporary dip in service during the transition period.

Another best practice is to have a standard format by which you communicate to the staff and vendor, including clear and consistent repetition of key elements, such as the business driver for outsourcing, why this particular vendor was selected, and the impact on the staff. In my workshops, I often get feedback that this exercise is one of the most valuable things covered.

Here is a partial checklist of important techniques for implementing a strong working relationship:

- Educate the supplier on corporate, business unit, and process strategies
- Set up orientation workshops for the supplier
- Form company and supplier teams
- Share supplier's knowledge and expertise with the company
- Establish face-to-face meetings, at least once every year

Phase 6: Management of the Relationship

The job of managing the vendor relationship never ends. It's an ongoing loop that includes several disciplines, including process monitoring, metrics tracking, capturing of results, measuring performance, and providing feedback.

There are various governance models you can use to ensure these processes are carried out. The one you choose depends on which type of vendor relationship you've established (provider, collaborator, or alliance).

There are at least six governance models currently in use, but the three most common include the following:

1. Process Owner
   - Establishes goals and objectives
   - Reviews process results
   - Reviews vendor service level agreements
   - Meets with vendor to resolve issues and improve communication
   - Ensures suboptimization is not occurring
2. Single Point of Contact
   - Provides a contact point for troubleshooting and problem solving
   - Assists support teams
   - Keeps vendor focused on delivery of service
   - Blocks vendor from directly selling to internal clients on services that might or might not be needed
3. Vendor Management Office (VMO)
   - Proactively aware of best vendors for specific services
   - Provides expertise and knowledge in selection and negotiation phase
   - Leverages services into acquisition
   - Fosters healthy competition
   - Provides pricing comparisons
   - Assists with managing multiple vendors in the same service area
   - Provides information on vendors with multiple contracts, resulting in optimal agreements and prices
   - Monitors metrics consistently across vendors
   - VMOs are not especially useful when vendor options are limited or static.

Of the clients I've worked with, I've seen people either decide on a single governance model, or create a hybrid model, whereby a single process owner is established, with points of contact managing the relationship on a day-to-day basis.

The vendor management office is growing in popularity. Just as the project management office has been established in some companies to develop best practices and advise companies on managing large and complex projects, the VMO plays a similar role. This is a centralized place for the company to turn to for people with specific skill sets in negotiations, relationship management, process management, and performance measurement and management.

As with vendor selection and contract negotiation, this phase should also be a team effort, involving the process owner, procurement, legal, finance, human resources and, increasingly, cyber security.

In this phase, you should also conduct regular reviews of vendor performance. The intensity and scope of the engagement will determine the frequency of the reviews, which can range from monthly to annually.

There are four primary categories of metrics. These include commitment, for which you would measure such components as quality and cost; flexibility, for which components include discounted pricing and acceptance of new requests; innovation, with components such as process improvement and market opportunities; and customer satisfaction, for which a key component is responsiveness.

The metrics you choose depend on whether the relationship is that of provider, collaborator, or alliance. For example, in a provider relationship, you would focus mainly on commitment and customer satisfaction, while in a collaborator relationship, you would also include flexibility and innovation.

I also encourage every organization to define a checklist to use during these reviews of subjective questions that can affect the overall relationship. For example, is the vendor culturally compatible with our company? What were the major sources of conflicts, and how were they handled?

To run a successful vendor performance review meeting, it's also important to develop all of the skill sets we've covered in this book, including negotiating, political savvy, conflict management, and influencing, as well as interpersonal and communication skills.

As the relationship unfolds, it's inevitable that it will endure ups and downs along the way. That's why I've developed a list of ten signs of distress to look for, so that you can take action before the relationship deteriorates to a danger point. These include the following:

1. Lack of responsiveness from vendor
2. Complaints from internal clients
3. New or unusual charges on a supplier's bill
4. Frequent performance issues with unsatisfactory explanations
5. Increased disagreement over small contractual issues
6. Demands from the vendor for additional charges for minor contract changes
7. Resistance to client requests that require some additional effort
8. Arguments over responsibility
9. Discord at governance meetings with vendor
10. Increased turnover on vendor and company teams

Phase 7: Evaluation of the Results

With all this information gathered, you can evaluate on a regular basis whether to continue the outsourcing relationship with the vendor. The decision on whether to change providers or move a function or process back in-house is not one that companies take lightly, as it entails a high cost.

Conclusion

I'm no soothsayer, but you don't need a highly calibrated crystal ball to forecast that companies will continue increasing their reliance on service providers, whether through full-fledged outsourcing relationships or one of the many as-a-service engagements.

For this reason, it's time to start treating vendor relationship management as a discipline, with skills and knowledge that will determine the success of the partnership. Whether you're aiming for a provider, collaborator, or alliance relationship, doing this right will be a source of competitive advantage.

Increasingly, when companies sign on the dotted line, they're going to want a partner that operates like a long-term solution provider—not just a vendor of products and services at a particular price. With the right skill set, we can develop the kinds of partnerships we want with service providers and realize the full set of benefits we expect.

Clearly, the trend will continue for more and more organizations to depend on vendors for many of their service needs. It will be critically important to any organization's success to retain a staff with the appropriate skills and knowledge to create and manage these vendor partnerships.

Top Ten

Ways to Improve Vendor Relationship Management

10. Move from a contract management to a relationship management mentality.
9. Transition from managing employees to managing the relationship.
8. Understand and differentiate between the goals and objectives of the organization and those of the vendor.

7. Utilize change management to transition employees to new roles.

6. Involve other corporate departments, including procurement, financial, legal, and people from departments involved with the process or function being outsourced.

5. Recognize and bridge the cultural differences gap between the organization and the vendor.

4. Improve vendor selection, contract development, and negotiation processes.

3. Be proactive in shaping a positive partnership and in recognizing when the relationship is in trouble.

2. Establish appropriate governance structures.

1. Create value for long-term competitive advantage.

Specific Actions I Will Take

- ▪
- ▪
- ▪

CHAPTER 11

Driving Change with Intent

The topic of change has been a constant theme throughout this book. Whether you are leading large-scale organizational transformation initiatives, a large or small project, or expanding the skills and capabilities of your workforce, you are embarking upon change.

Today's business world is one of change—constant, inevitable, unending change. And in this world, the *only* people who will survive are those who learn to turn on a dime. It's true for companies, as well—those who effectively create a culture of change are the ones rising to the top of the marketplace.

Nowhere is this more true than within the IT organization. Not only do IT leaders need to embrace change, but in many cases, they're also the ones shouldered with the responsibility of making change happen throughout the enterprise. Look at what IT does every day—whether it's helping the company develop more innovative products or services, hone the bottom line, streamline the supply chain, or comply with new regulations, the projects that IT is involved in always involve aspects of change—to people, processes, systems, or all three.

You might wonder then, why IT leaders don't spend time focused on the possibility of these types of changes not taking place, especially considering the risks involved—the risk of delays or running over budget, the risk that the new tool or system doesn't get used as planned or doesn't meet the business objective. The fact is, change doesn't just happen. Like an event or project, successful change has to be planned, structured, monitored, and led, with purpose and intent. But that's not how change is usually treated.

From what we've seen in our years of working with IT, most CIOs and other IT leaders are very aware of change. But they simply don't have the know-how to manage it through to successful completion. They might put a risk mitigation strategy in place, involving plans to address the more obvious risks, and they might do some contingency planning and preparation. But only rarely do we see an IT organization apply the same amount of rigor toward planning for and driving the components of change necessary for success.

We've all seen what happens when change goes unmanaged. The targeted users of the system never really commit to the project or embrace their new responsibilities. People become disengaged and even hostile, refusing to get involved with any stage of the project or even sabotaging the effort. Excuses are given: "Well, if they would just go to training," or, "We delivered exactly what they asked for on time and on budget. I don't know why they aren't seeing the results stated in their business case."

In some cases, we've heard IT leaders complain that even though they've sent out e-mails and memos regarding a big initiative and all the changes it entails, people still don't seem to get it. "I've communicated about this for six months," they say, "and people say they never heard about it!" It's no wonder most organizations believe their organizational transformation efforts and change initiatives are only marginally successful at best.

It's up to IT to play this role, to help the people affected by the system understand, accept, and ultimately embrace the changes wrought by the initiative. And the leaders and organizations that aren't doing this—and developing the skills and tools to make change happen—will simply be seen as ineffective, costly, and, ultimately, replaceable.

In this chapter, we hope to pass along some of what we've learned about what change leadership and a culture of change can look like. Anyone can do it, as long as they know about the dynamics of change and learn the structures, tools, and skills to lead and manage it.

Defining Terms

Throughout this chapter, we use terminology that's a bit different from other chapters in the book. For example, we use the term, *target users* to refer to anyone affected by the change, at any level, whether it's a change to their business process, the technology they use, the way they behave, or the nature of their relationships.

There are also three essential roles that need to be filled, both by IT staff and by others in the business community. It's up to the IT group to identify the right people to play these roles. The three roles include change leader, change agent, and change advocate. Change leaders are the people who sponsor and validate the project that's causing the change to occur. There are usually a number of individuals assigned to this role, and it's important that they be placed broadly and deeply throughout the organization.

The second—change agents, are the people who plan, facilitate, and implement key change activities. And the last—change advocates (also called *opinion leaders*), are the people required to achieve successful change. I explain these roles more specifically later in the chapter.

The Components of Change

To start down the path of becoming an effective leader of change, it's important to understand the components of

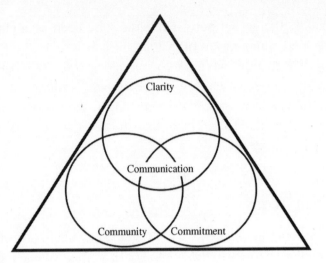

FIGURE 11.1 Components of Change

change—commitment, community, and clarity—as well as the glue that brings them all together: communication.

O&A has a simple model (see Figure 11.1) to help you understand these components and how they interact. Notice first that change is represented with a triangle and three conjoined circles, not with squares connected by arrows. This is purposely done because the components are all interrelated, and they're also not linear. While there are checklists within each component, it's not like a flowchart, whereby you close the book on one task and then move on to the next. Change is not linear; it's a dynamic process. Let's move through these components, starting with commitment.

Achieving Commitment Is Essential for Sustaining Change

When thinking about change it is important to understand the difference between compliance and commitment. Compliance means going along with a recommendation or new process without really believing in it. It's when you're mandated into

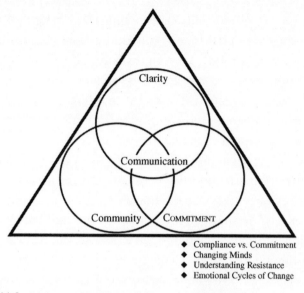

◆ Compliance vs. Commitment
◆ Changing Minds
◆ Understanding Resistance
◆ Emotional Cycles of Change

FIGURE 11.2 Components of Change—Commitment

changing your behavior without changing your mindset. And it means it wouldn't take much to knock you off course or make you go back to your old ways when no one is looking.

Commitment means being bound emotionally and intellectually to a course of action or to another person. It leads to sustained behavioral change. Commitment is very personal—no one can force another person to commit to something; people have to make that jump themselves. And when they do, they're full participants—they believe in what they're doing and where they're heading, and they're intent on completing the journey (see Figure 11.2).

We've heard some people say, "You don't need commitment at work," or, "If commitment requires my 'soul,' I won't give my soul to my job," or, "All you need is a commitment for compliance." These are nice catchphrases, and maybe you agree with one or all of them, but we certainly don't. If the definition of commitment involves buy-in, then you've got to align your mind, body, and soul to the effort.

207

Most of the time, without even thinking about it, IT leaders get compliance rather than commitment from target users. And then they wonder why, six months later, people aren't embracing the new process or system they delivered. It's because they weren't truly committed! The fact is that failing to achieve commitment is the single most important reason why IT organizations cannot sustain change.

It's true that gaining commitment from others is a difficult challenge, primarily because you can't change another person's mind; they have to do it for themselves. An individual's mindset involves his internal beliefs, philosophies, and values. This is classified information and difficult to assess. But while achieving true commitment can be challenging, the payoff is huge. Imagine if every team member and user of the new system completely bought in to the new features, functions, tools, and processes. Think about how easy training would be, how great it would be that instead of people complaining about the change, they're providing feedback on continuous improvement. They're tolerating the bumps in the road because they believe the end goal is worth the wait. Isn't this worth your time and energy? Focus on achieving the commitment level required for your project to succeed.

There are times that full commitment isn't necessary. In some cases—say, a new time-tracking system—the target user might grumpily comply with a new process because doing otherwise would be personally detrimental; in this example, she wouldn't get paid. But many initiatives bear high risk for the company, not the target user directly, and failure to get them in place could turn into costly debacles, affecting the top and bottom lines. To know which you need—commitment or compliance—just ask yourself what's the risk if target users don't get on board?

In other cases, there's simply not enough time to go for full commitment at the beginning of the project. But that doesn't mean you should stop and give up. In these cases, it's important to work purposefully toward the goal of commitment over time to secure it.

When working toward commitment, it's important to remember that resistance is a natural part of change. Depending on the severity as perceived by the individual, it's as if a survival instinct kicks in, and the feeling of loss can be overwhelming. People's natural inclination is to protect themselves, preserve their competence, maintain their comfort zone, or stay in line with their personal values. Everyone has an individual capacity for change, and when that limit is reached, there may be feelings of frustration and feeling overwhelmed, with potentially diminished returns.

Most IT leaders just ignore resistance, or worse, say things like, "Just get with the program," driving people further into resistance or, at best, compliance. As an effective leader of change, you should expect resistance. You should never be surprised when it occurs. In fact, we challenge you to go so far as to anticipate it. Set up a safe environment to explore it. Resistance brings new information and tells you that the individual has energy invested. Your job, as a leader of change, is to turn that energy from a negative state to a positive one. In doing so, you allow for an opportunity to build commitment.

To better understand resistance and other natural responses to change, we talk about the psychology of change during our Leading Change workshop. Studies have shown that people who are responding to unwanted or unwelcome change tend to move through what we call the emotional cycles of change, which are similar to the Kübler-Ross model of the five stages of grief—denial, anger, bargaining, depression, and acceptance.

To lead people through change, it's important to identify where target users are in the cycle and know how to help them move into the acceptance stage as quickly as possible. The following are the emotional cycles of change and a brief word on how to handle them:

- *Immobilization*. This is brought on by anxiety, fear, and confusion. The best approach is to accept and acknowledge these emotions, while repeatedly offering brief, clear information and support.
- *Denial.* At this stage, people are unable to accurately absorb information or participate appropriately. The best approach is to continue providing information and team them up with someone who's moved to the acceptance phase.
- *Anger.* Don't take this phase personally. Allow target users to vent these emotions, while listening carefully for issues that are real and need to be addressed.
- *Bargaining*. At this stage, it's important to help individuals get involved in the changes and feel a part of the action. You can listen to people's suggestions, being careful to consider which ones actually fit, while dismissing those that don't. You can start setting specific tasks with specific time frames and establish consequences of noncompliance.
- *Depression*. People in this stage need support and empathy, as well as encouragement to take responsibility. You can break tasks into small segments and reinforce success, while talking to individuals and setting up forums in which they can air their concerns and provide input.
- *Testing*. Individuals in this stage begin to get involved with the changes happening around them. It's important to establish clear boundaries and parameters while helping people explore realistic options.
- *Acceptance*. People are seeing the potentials within the change and are adjusting or adapting to it. People's efforts need to be recognized, and progress should be acknowledged.

Change Takes a Community

The second component of change is community, because driving change is more akin to a symphony orchestra than a soloist. In other words, it takes different people collaborating together in diverse roles to make it work. It's up to IT leaders to identify and engage the right people to play the carefully scripted roles mentioned earlier in the chapter, those of change leader, change advocate, and change agent (see Figure 11.3).

We call this community of people the *transition structure.* Some companies formalize these three roles by creating a change management office. For example, one global retailer that embarked on a $650 million project over six years created a three-person change management office as part of its transition structure. The important thing is not how you structure these roles, but that you make change purposeful and don't leave it to chance.

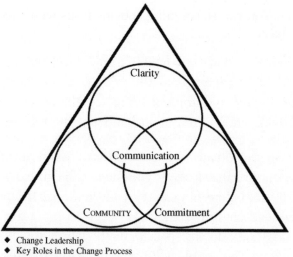

♦ Change Leadership
♦ Key Roles in the Change Process
♦ Transition Structures
♦ Network of Resources

FIGURE 11.3 Components of Change—Community

Change Leader

Let's start with the change leaders. These are the people who sponsor and validate the project that's causing the change to occur. The people who should play this role include anyone with target users in their organization. They need to convincingly portray to target users the reasons for the change and paint a vivid picture of what the end state looks like. They need to sponsor not only the goal but also the journey toward the goal.

To do that, change leaders need to outline for target users how the change will be accomplished, especially given their regular work and current culture. This requires the ability to speak passionately, think strategically, and plan tactically. All along the way, these leaders need to remain visible, provide unwavering support, and inject energy when momentum wanes. They can't just pop out on occasion to champion the cause. Staying close to target users is essential, as these leaders need to anticipate their needs and motivations, orchestrate people dynamics, and earn the trust of the people they work with.

Change Agent

The second role that's essential to a successful change initiative is that of the change agent—the people responsible for planning, facilitating, and implementing key change activities. The three activities most closely associated with this role are:

1. *Connecting.* Change agents have to connect well with clients, peers, and change leaders. They need to be trusted, respected, and likable before they can exert any influence. In other words, they need charisma. They also need to put aside personal agendas and exhibit respect for the people they work with.
2. *Engaging.* The people in this role need to facilitate conversation and exploration of the vision, while also making changes practical.

3. *Guiding*. Change agents need to foster synergy among target users, guide the plans and activities associated with change, identify issues among the group, and help change leaders adjust direction when these issues become acute.

For example, when leadership teams send out inconsistent messages about a change, it is incumbent on the change agent to point that out and help the team frame a standard message. When change leaders aren't accessible enough—it is the change agent who needs to raise awareness of this and make suggestions about how to be more visible, like stopping by work areas or conducting listening sessions.

Change Advocate

The third important role is that of change advocate (also called *opinion leaders*). The people in this role can make or break the change effort because they have such strong influence over other people, both positive and negative.

To identify change advocates, IT needs to map out the political landscape and understand the influence dynamics at play— who is affected by the change, who has indirect and direct power, who supports the change, and who doesn't. We've covered all the skills required to understand the political landscape in Chapter 8 on sharpening your political savvy.

It's important to identify opinion leaders who are positive about the change, because they can help move things along more smoothly. But it's just as important to engage the negative influencers, because they could otherwise sabotage the effort. To get change advocates on board, IT needs to forge an understanding of their values and issues, their personality type, and communication style, as well as the "what's in it for me" factor, or WIIFM. We then need to provide the change advocates with the information they need so they can get other people on board and request their assistance in making changes more visible.

Clarity Precedes Activity

The third component of change is clarity, and there are two important elements involved in achieving clarity: making the case for change and ensuring the path forward is clear (see Figure 11.4).

Making the Case for Change

It takes more than a good idea to inspire people to commit to change. To illustrate this point, we use the analogy of a burning platform—many people won't jump into the unknown until they're really feeling the heat. Establishing that burning platform means understanding and being able to convey the business imperative for the change. In other words, why is the change necessary, and why does it make good business sense?

We define *business imperative* as being a situation in which the cost of the status quo is greater than the cost of change. To

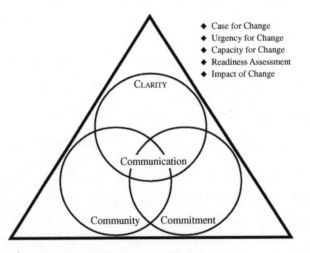

FIGURE 11.4 Components of Change—Clarity

get target users to make the leap to committing to change, the pain of the current situation has to be greater than the pain of making the change. This means that IT needs to be able to convey that the current state is no longer viable and why this is so—whether it's a new competitor entering the market, shifting economic conditions, changes in customer preferences, or something else. Typical business imperatives fall into one of several categories, including strategic, financial, customer, operational, employee, or regulatory.

Once you've clearly defined the business imperative, an accurate portrayal of the future needs to be painted—what does it look like, and what are the steps involved in getting there? What are the risks involved, and how will those risks be managed? How will target users be supported along the way?

Target users need to personally and emotionally connect with the change, which means IT needs to be able to clearly articulate how the change will ultimately benefit them—again, addressing the WIIFM. This involves putting yourself in their position, understanding their resistance and talking to them—in terms they'll understand—about what they stand to lose or gain with the impending change. They need to make a personal connection to what they have at stake, both positive and negative.

To drive this point home, I use a cliff analogy. Picture someone standing on a mountain peak, looking at another beautiful peak in the distance. How do you get the person to move from one peak to the other? As already described, the person first needs the motivation to want to move—the business imperative. But even when the person is committed, there's still a huge chasm she's got to get across, and she'll need support, guidance, and lots of other help getting over the rocky and treacherous path.

If you can clearly articulate the business imperative and put it into terms that speak to the target user, you can more quickly achieve commitment. People who have a *why* will do almost any *how*.

Ensuring the Path Forward Is Clear

Obstacles are inevitable in change initiatives. It is important to anticipate where those obstacles lie and how to eliminate them. That means assessing the impact the change is likely to have on various target groups, as well as the organization's readiness to absorb those impacts. During O&A's Leading Change workshop, people are exposed to charts and checklists they can use to make these two separate assessments. The following is an overview of those tools.

Assessing the impact of change involves defining who the various stakeholder groups are and then understanding how the change affects them in terms of low, medium, or high impact. You can do this by analyzing the scope of the change, the amount of change these groups will endure, and how quickly the changes have to be implemented.

Some categories to consider in regard to impact include:

- *Knowledge and skill.* To what degree will they need to change their knowledge and capabilities to complete required job functions?
- *Processes.* Will they need to change the detailed steps of the work they perform?
- *Organizational structure.* How much will formal reporting structures within the organization change?
- *Relationships.* What changes will occur to the way groups and individuals relate to one another in day-to-day work, including teaming changes, political affiliations, and so forth?
- *Culture.* What impact will the change have on basic values and beliefs?
- *Technology.* What changes will happen to the technology used in day-to-day work?

Once you've identified areas of medium and high impact, we recommend that you conduct a change readiness assessment. Change readiness is a measure of how well the environment is set up to succeed with change—whether the conditions for success exist. Readiness depends upon a number of factors, including:

- Has a clear business case been defined?
- Is cohesive leadership in place?
- Is there an attitude of willingness and respect for those leading the change?
- Are there sufficient resources for the change?
- Was the change designed in an open and collaborative way?

Looking at these readiness factors, you can determine which of them pose medium or high risk to the change initiative and then develop a risk mitigation strategy that will set up the change initiative for more likely success.

Messaging the Change

The last component of change is communication—the glue that holds the entire change initiative together (see Figure 11.5). It's how target users are supported through the emotional cycles of change. It's how commitment to the change initiative is inspired. It's how the change leadership community effectively plays their various roles. And it's how clarity is achieved to clear the obstacles preventing change.

And yet while leaders spend untold time discussing, debating, strategizing, and planning, they spend little to no time effectively communicating those same strategies and plans.

We often hear, "There's no time for communication." But when you think about how much time is wasted with rumors, speculation, and worry over what's going to happen or what's around the corner—if that time were translated into productivity loss, imagine what the figure would be!

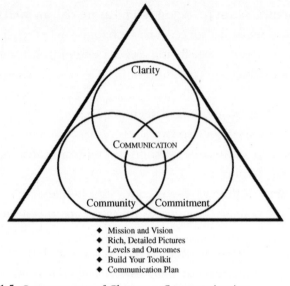

- ◆ Mission and Vision
- ◆ Rich, Detailed Pictures
- ◆ Levels and Outcomes
- ◆ Build Your Toolkit
- ◆ Communication Plan

FIGURE 11.5 Components of Change—Communication

Surprisingly, in our world of people interacting with people, communication is typically the weakest link. This may be because we all assume that communication is obvious. But it's absolutely not when it comes to communicating change. In times of change, everything that is said by the leaders of change sets an expectation about what the future may hold. People are waiting, wondering, reluctant, and potentially fearful, which can incite a number of emotions. These emotional states will affect your ability to drive productivity within your organization. That's why it's so essential to drive your communications intentionally and with purpose. And remember, communication is not an event; it's an accompaniment to life and to your change initiative.

Here's a good example of successful communication: When there's a significant systems outage, one of our clients applies more staff resources to communicating what's going on with the outage than they do to the technical fix of the problem. Their clients appreciate the communication so much that they actually think the problems are being solved faster than if all those people were actually working on the outage.

When creating your communication strategy, keep in mind that there are five different levels of communication. While many IT leaders use just two levels, the three less-used levels are the ones most effective at getting people to change. The levels most IT leaders use to communicate are one-way techniques, such as town halls, presentations, memos, and videos to communicate in a unilateral direction with project stakeholders. Some might also employ two-way methods such as small-group meetings, breakout sessions, and facilitated Q&As to encourage dialogue.

However, inspiring change requires a third level of communication, called *identifying implications.* In this level, target users meet and have interactive group discussions about the implications of the change. Groups can be large or small, but the most important exploration is done with just the work team and the immediate supervisor. This interactive, multidirectional style encourages people to voice their concerns, which helps reveal obstacles that must be overcome.

A fourth level is *gaining commitment,* and it involves multiple small-group meetings that allow people to sort out their inner feelings and choices, as well as provide private introspective time. This type of communication encourages people to develop a personal connection with the change at hand. This isn't a one-time meeting; rather, it requires multiple returns to the discussion with peers, immediate supervisors, or change leaders.

In the last level of communication—*altering behavior*—leaders demonstrate the new behavior that they expect from target users. They may need to use training, coaching, and feedback mechanisms over time to ensure that the new behaviors stick. They should also provide plenty of opportunities for practice and learning and may need to reinforce desired behavior with policy or systems changes.

If you've ever found yourself wondering why a particular person or group doesn't seem to be listening to you, take a look at what level of communication you're employing. Better yet, determine which stage of the emotional cycle of change the person is in and you'll get an even better picture of what's going on. If you adjust your communication style, you'll have a better chance of getting through.

And remember that communication doesn't always have to be dry and direct. If you've ever taken a writing course, or even read the sports pages, you know that metaphors and analogies go a long way toward helping people visualize what you're trying to get across. This is particularly true when you're trying to convey what the future will look like. Try using narrative to describe a day-in-the-life-of the future, or anecdotes to describe the kind of behavior you want to see. There are rich communication techniques to convey what you see the future sounding like, looking like, and feeling like.

Conclusion

If there's one thing to remember from this chapter, it's that change doesn't just happen. It needs to be driven with purpose and intent. And for a change initiative to succeed, IT leaders, as leaders of change, need to understand and manage the four components of change—commitment, community, clarity, and communication. Don't even think of embarking on a change initiative without using the tools, skills, and techniques discussed in this chapter.

Many very smart people ignore these facts, spending numerous hours talking about their IT projects while avoiding the topic of change like the plague. Project status meetings usually include discussions about scope, requirements, development, testing, infrastructure, processes, training, budget, resources, and business cases. Though these topics are important, so are the topics of change impact, communication, readiness, behavioral obstacles, risks and mitigating strategies, and commitment!

Throughout this book, we've challenged you to adopt new mindsets, grow additional skills, and apply new personal toolkits to help you and your organization succeed in this profession. And it's all about change. You need to establish a culture of change to ensure that both you and the organization you lead are prepared for the future.

Top Ten

Ways to Drive Change with Intent

10. Every IT project involves change.
 9. People who have a *why* will do almost any *how*.
 8. Know the difference between commitment and compliance.
 7. Speak passionately, think strategically, and plan tactically.
 6. Conduct impact and readiness assessments.
 5. Only *I* can change *my* mindset and *my* behaviors.
 4. Use five levels of communication.
 3. Know the emotional cycles of change.
 2. Communication is not an event.
 1. Change is personal.

Specific Actions I Will Take

-
-
-

CHAPTER 12

Putting the Book into Action: Stories from the Trenches

How many times have you read a compelling management book and then—after looking up from its pages and walking through the hallways of your workplace—thought: "Okay, where do I start?" Or even, "That would never work here."

That is not how we roll, here at Ouellette & Associates. Our goal is to always provide tangible, actionable, real-world insights that can be applied immediately. As a busy leader, you don't have the time for theory and generic concepts. You need proven strategies and approaches that will help you change the mindset and develop the skill set your people need to help them become trusted partners who are an integral part of the business.

We're proud to say we've seen just these kinds of positive impacts occurring within the more than 3,000 IT organizations we're fortunate enough to work with, across a wide range of industries. We've seen it at St. Luke's Health System, whose transformation into a health care network depended on close alignment and real relationships among physicians, staff, and IT. With our help, the CIO led her staff—as well as key stakeholders from the health care network—through a cultural shift, from one of IT disconnect to real IT engagement. With the new relationship between IT and its clients, St. Luke's is now ready to face the daunting challenges that lie ahead in health care.

We've also seen it at Marriott, whose fast, organic growth—as well as more technologically sophisticated guests—required more effective deployment of technology and a strong partnership between IT and the business. Working with the CIO, we watched the IT organization at this global hospitality giant become as business-savvy as the clients they worked with, and shift from enabling business strategy, to helping shape it.

And we've seen it at Bowdoin College, a top college in Maine that wanted to become one of the most technically advanced liberal arts institutions in the country. The CIO called upon us to introduce a service mindset to his staff, as well as teach skills in change management and marketing IT. Today, Bowdoin's IT group is busy supporting the facilities, academic, and business areas of the college, as well as conducting business process reviews. Thanks to the transformation, the CIO is proud to note that the college is now a "change-positive organization."

But don't take our word for it—hear it from our clients, themselves, in this compilation of three CIOs who have applied the teachings of this book to transform their IT culture and to prepare their IT staff to succeed in an increasingly complex, ever-changing business environment.

A Newly Consultative IT Function Helps Drive St. Luke's Health System Transformation

Nearly every industry is facing massive change today, but none so much as health care. With spiraling costs, increased regulations, and government mandates for electronic health records, health care providers are under immense pressure to increase the quality of care, boost patient outcomes, and improve data access—all in a streamlined, efficient way.

St. Luke's Health System in Idaho is no exception. When Adrienne Edens joined the organization as CIO in early 2008, it was transitioning from its roots as a hospital system to an integrated delivery network. So not only was it facing the traditional challenges of a health care provider, but it also needed to change the entire way it functioned.

"We were moving into a different business model," Edens says. "We needed much more alignment between the physicians and the hospitals, we needed to produce more quality metrics, and we needed integrated systems that would help people see the bigger picture and help us coordinate patient care."

At the same time, cost pressures were mounting, she says. "Every dollar the organization spends on IT is money it can't spend on a new piece of diagnostic equipment or a renovation of a patient care floor."

For the transformation to be successful, Edens determined that IT also needed a makeover. Rather than engaging in long-range strategic planning, many hospital units were accustomed to acquiring applications and technology without considering the needs of other areas, such as financial, acute care, or clinical diagnostics.

"We needed IT to get closer to the clients to help them choose something that could expand to suit new markets and future needs," Edens says. The organization also needed IT support for new physicians joining the network and enabling enterprise access to patient data.

A Cultural Shift

"Meeting these new requirements entailed an entirely new mindset and culture within IT," Edens says. At the time, business clients reported frustration in their attempts to engage with IT, including unreturned phone calls and e-mails. Even when they did form a good relationship with a particular IT professional, it was only a matter of time before the person left to work on a different project and was no longer able to help.

Meanwhile, on the IT side, the staff felt disconnected from the work of the clients they were supporting, confused about their job descriptions and had very low morale. Frequent reassignments resulted in constant disruption to any connection they could forge with clients. The unhappiness showed in the department's job satisfaction scores: "IT had the lowest scores of any group at St. Luke's," Edens says.

One major reason for the gulf between IT and the business was the structure of the IT organization, which was aligned around IT functions and activities, not the business. Not only were the various technology groups cut off from their clients, they were also isolated from each other. "They didn't cooperate or coordinate their work well, even to the point of getting in each other's way when it came to getting something accomplished," she says.

Lastly, while highly skilled technologically, individual IT professionals did not have the skills to engage with their business clients. "They didn't know what to do or what they could say," Edens says.

Addressing the Issues

The first thing Edens did was restructure the organization by aligning it around business needs. Instead of organizing teams around IT functions, she created customer-facing service teams, including teams for acute care, clinical diagnostics, ambulatory services, and business services.

She also turned to Ouellette & Associates to guide the IT staff toward becoming a service-oriented, consultative organization. After all, Edens says, "How do you deliver good service when you don't know what that is?"

At first, the Consulting Skills workshops were offered to a select number of analysts and project managers from a variety of facilities and sites across St. Luke's. Soon, however, it was apparent that the entire staff would benefit from the training, which happened over the course of a year. Also, the operations and help desk staff completed the Achieving IT Service Excellence workshop.

St. Luke's leadership group also spent a day learning how to push the changes further and deeper into the organization. And Edens invited IT executives, physicians, and some key directors from some of the business departments to take the service workshop together. The goal was to better understand the business's expectations of IT and the day-to-day needs that weren't being met. "These were our key stakeholders, so spending two days with them helped build relationships, as well as an appreciation for how committed we were to providing great service. It got them to see us differently, that we were willing to change and improve our service."

Breaking Old Models

As with any major transformation, St. Luke's ran into challenges along the way. One was breaking the assignment-oriented management style that IT was accustomed to, as well as the mindset that only the service desk should interact with clients. "They were used to being told what to do and not stepping outside the boundaries," Edens says. "Some people felt hesitant to just charge in there."

The IT organization was also unaccustomed to thinking of itself as a unified team but rather as individual units that were sometimes at odds with each other. "We had to focus on becoming team members and working better together," Edens says.

These problems were worked through by customizing the workshops and enabling participants to role-play difficult and even confrontational situations. "They needed to practice how to engage in constructive dialogue to solve problems and address the requirements but present different options," Edens says.

According to Edens, IT now has a whole new understanding of the value it offers to physicians, hospital staff, and patients. "It was a revelation," Edens says. "They realized they didn't feel connected enough to the business and that they weren't satisfied with the former quality of work they were doing."

Relationships with the business were also strengthened. "They could develop permanent working relationships and provide ongoing, committed support to help their clients get more out of the systems they had," Edens says.

Networking with other IT staff members was an important side benefit, as well. "The group really listened to one another and began to understand the issues that the infrastructure team had versus application support versus the help desk," Edens says. "Making sure the groups were mixed allowed them to get to know their colleagues and establish contacts."

Ah-Ha Moments

According to Edens, the transformation has resulted in more satisfied IT staff and business clients. In a recent employee engagement survey, Edens says, two IT teams were rated in the highest Tier 1 category, and two more were rated as Tier 2.

IT is also helping St. Luke's with its own business transformation. For example, an IT team was established for developing onboarding processes for new physicians, and the ambulatory team is now supporting an IT steering committee created to ensure enterprise-wide access to patient information.

By engaging in more strategic project planning and enabling better project outcomes, IT has also helped raise productivity and lower costs. A good example is when St. Luke's radiology department decided it needed a new electronic picture archiving and communication system (PACS). Rather than simply fulfilling the request, IT took a more strategic route, working with physicians and imaging leaders to plan an enterprise image system to store all images in one place, provide web-based viewing access, and include voice recognition for recording results. The voice recognition system is now saving $72,000 per month in transcription costs and has reduced turnaround time on results from nine hours to one.

From the clients' perspective, this experience represents a dramatic change. "When we first started our relationship with IT, they lacked an understanding of just how integral they are to patient care," says Ralph Lundquist, director of medical imaging at St. Luke's. "The radiologists can't do anything without the IT department, and once they adopted that understanding, they became more accountable and sensitive to the overall impact they have and the responsibility they share with us."

Today, Lundquist says, if the PACS system goes down, the IT team is right there. "They'll stay on board 36 hours if they have to, they're that dedicated to their job and taking care of patients."

Dr. John Waltz, department chair of radiology, agrees that the transformation has been exceptional. "Before, our interaction was more fragmented and disconnected, but now we see the PACS team every day," he says. "I'm absolutely dependent on them for everything I do, from the time I come in, to the time I leave. They get that, too—they're not IT guys hiding in the closet, throwing switches and pounding on keyboards."

In another case, when discussing enhancements to the surgical supply processes, IT sat down with the business stakeholders, and the group realized together that the project was far bigger and more complex than what they originally thought.

"By mapping everything out, everyone got a much better picture of the project scope," Edens says. The group developed a joint presentation on the lessons learned from this process and presented it at the next quarterly leadership meeting, explaining why they needed to recast the project.

IT also feels free to proactively suggest new ideas to business clients. One IT team decided it needed to help simplify access to clinical systems. It brought in a vendor to demo a solution, got sponsorship from the clinical team, started partnering on a proof of concept, and developed a test system. "This was not the business coming to us, saying, 'I want this,'" Edens says. "Our engineering group is now more innovative and feels comfortable coming up with uses for technology they think has applicability to solving business problems."

Communications are also much improved. IT service teams now schedule regular monthly status meetings with their business partners. "They used to plow along and get the work done, but now, they're communicating the progress they're making and asking how they can work more closely with the business," Edens says.

The staff is also conducting internal hindsight reviews after projects are finished. When discussing something that didn't go well, they focus on the process, not what individual people did or did not do. "It's something the group hadn't done before, but since they all took the workshop, it makes it easier."

One last benefit, she says, is that the IT staff now knows they don't need to have the answers all the time. "They used to struggle between providing good technology advice and doing what the customer wanted," she says. "Now they can think through the situation and work with their business counterparts to come up with a better solution."

Continuing the Momentum

For the future, Edens foresees further O&A workshops in Partnering Skills, Strengthening the IT/Client Relationship, and even Marketing IT. She also asked O&A to conduct a Leading Change in IT workshop for a group composed of IT staff and IT department leaders. "We have a lot of new technology we're going to be implementing and new initiatives we're undertaking," she says. "We need to get clarity around the types of change we'll be implementing and how to sustain it."

The IT transformation, Edens says, has changed the type of work that IT is able to do.

"The relationships are in place, and we can conduct more honest and thoughtful dialogue of what we're doing," she says. "We're more tuned in to what our priorities are and what kind of focus is needed for us to do a good job."

Or, as Dr. Greg Jones at St. Luke's puts it, "When IT creates efficiencies in the care process, the patient is healthier and happier."

At Marriott, a Transformed IT-Business Relationship Is the Underpinning for Hospitality Giant's Success

The mid-1990s were a busy time for Marriott International, Inc. The now $11 billion global lodging and hospitality giant was acquiring other major hotel companies, such as the Ritz-Carlton Hotel Company and Renaissance Hotel Group; introducing new brands; entering new markets and exiting others; and opening new properties at a fierce pace around the world. By 1998, it had opened its 1,500th hotel—quite a feat, considering its portfolio had reached the 100-property mark just 17 years before.

"We were growing organically—adding companies, rooms and concepts," says Carl Wilson, executive vice president and CIO at Marriott, which has surpassed its fiftieth anniversary in the hotel business and now operates more than 3,400 properties in 70 countries and territories.

That success, however, could not have been achieved without developing a whole new approach to effectively deploying technology, as well as creating a strong partnership between the information resources (IR) organization and the business. "Our sheer growth meant the old practices would not allow us to be successful," says Wilson, who joined Marriott in 1997.

At the time, technology was also moving from the back offices of Marriott, into the hands of customer-facing employees, and it was a bigger part of the day-to-day lives of Marriott's customers, whether they were booking a room or in the middle of their hotel stay. "We had to make sure we were staying current and meeting the expectations of our guests," Wilson says.

With the introduction of Marriott.com—which Wilson points out is where many guests are first introduced to Marriott—it also became clear that IR could become a driver of top-line growth.

With the increasingly powerful role technology could play for businesses at the time, a role reversal was beginning to occur at Marriott in regard to business strategy and the systems that supported it. "Traditionally, if you asked a CIO what the role of technology was in the company, they'd say it was to enable and support the business strategy," Wilson says. "But that's an old paradigm—not only does it enable strategy, but it can also shape the strategy of the company. There are things you can do with technology that you cannot do without it."

A New Role for IR

With all this in mind, it became vitally important to Marriott's success that the IR organization embrace a new role: To help the company stay relevant and effective, through the use of technology. "For a company like Marriott, technology is a part of the actual service you provide to the end customer, so it has to be at the forefront of your capabilities, and it has to be effective," Wilson says. "Otherwise, the whole Marriott brand would be damaged."

To do that, Wilson knew he needed to change the culture, mindset, and skill set of the IR group and forge a stronger partnership between IR and the business. While both the business and IR were highly capable and had accomplished many things, he says, they lacked a common language to work together effectively. "The relationship wasn't nearly as effective as it needed to be," he says.

Nor, he says, was project management. "Projects took longer and cost more than they needed to, and in the end, they didn't always fulfill the business needs." Lacking a strategic approach, projects tended to be centered on creating spot solutions to individual problems rather than holistic business solutions.

Not to mention, in a company whose motto is "Spirit to Serve" (as well as the title of founder Bill Marriott's book, which is recommended reading for all new hires) it had become critical that the IR organization provided the same level of service to its business clients that they, in turn, were expected to provide hotel guests. "A lot of what Marriott is known for is the friendliness and helpfulness of our people," Wilson says.

The very first thing that needed to happen, Wilson says, was to bulk up the business's trust and confidence in IR by overhauling key corporate systems and improving operational weaknesses, such as system reliability rates. "If you can't do the basics well, you won't be given the opportunity to do more value-added work," Wilson says.

Wilson also contacted Ouellette & Associates to teach the IR staff new skills in the areas of IT service, consulting skills, and marketing. Wilson had previously worked with O&A when he was CIO at Georgia-Pacific Corp., where he also completed a successful IT transformation. He distributed dozens of O&A's books to top IR leaders, who took the service models presented in the books and workshops and wove them into IR's work processes.

The IR staff also received a framed copy of Wilson's 10 operational values, honed through his years as a CIO. These values outline how people, product, and processes will work together, Wilson says, and remind associates to work constantly with business partners to understand their rapidly changing needs and develop new, value-added services to meet those needs. "It's the first thing I share with people I'll be working with," he says. "It's the basis of my leadership style."

On the Same Page

To strengthen the IR organization's business acumen, Wilson launched an initiative to educate them on the hospitality industry. "You sometimes hear IT people say that the business needs to understand technology better. But we took it the other way— we have to understand the business and then take the technology to them and communicate in their language," he says. "Over time, we can teach them our language."

Wilson also created an internal IR consulting group, staffed with people with previous experience as business consultants. And very importantly, he began requiring that every major project had a full-time business and IR leader working together as a team. Both leaders were jointly accountable for achieving business benefits. "It just doesn't work when the IT function tries to transform itself unless you bring the customers and business partners along with them," he says.

To improve project management, Wilson also implemented a professional project certification program, for both IR and business people to attend, side by side. This had an immediate impact, he says. "It created a common way to manage projects and communicate with one another," he says. "Everyone was on the same page—it was no longer *we* versus *they*—it was *us*."

True Business Integration

All this work was so successful that, according to Bill Shaw, chief operating officer at Marriott, it became hard to discern in business meetings which people were from IR and which were from a business unit.

Before, Shaw says, a lot of technology people were not comfortable with the business because they didn't understand how it worked. At the same time, he says, business employees weren't comfortable with technology, either. "It was a matter of getting both sides to work more closely together and make sure that on every project there was a business person responsible for the outcome, as well as someone from the IT function," he says. "It's like building a hotel—you can't just hand the project over to the construction group; you need someone from each side there."

Particularly as more reservation business moves to the Internet, IR is a crucial presence at corporate strategy meetings. "We make sure Carl and his team are in these meetings, to know what the competition is doing and how that would affect our business," Shaw says. "They're keeping an eye on what's going on in the Internet world and since they also understand the business, they can see where the risks are and what the opportunities might be."

Not only does IR now have a prominent seat at the executive level, there is not a single decision-making body within Marriott of which Wilson or one of his direct reports is not a part. "We are truly integrated," Wilson says.

Indeed, in the last 14 years, Wilson has seen IR become essential to the operations of Marriott. The business now depends on technology to drive its ability to grow, from revenue management, to customer relationship management, to reservations. Case in point is the Marriott.com web site, now worth $6 billion in revenue and the company's lowest-cost distribution channel. "We've seen our technology move from the back office to the front desk, and now into hotel rooms and even our guests' homes and offices as people book online," he says. "If we're going to continue to be relevant, it's important that the technology meets our guests where they are," Wilson says.

The IR staff also seems to be happy with the relationship. Turnover throughout Marriott is extremely low. Through his tenure at many organizations, more than 20 of Wilson's own direct reports have moved on to become CIOs themselves. The IR organization has earned multiple awards, including a place on *Computerworld*'s annual Best Places to Work in IT list since 2003 and Top 12 Green IT companies since 2008. Wilson himself has earned a long list of awards and accolades, including induction into the prestigious *CIO Magazine* CIO Hall of Fame.

The entire transformation took about five years, Wilson says, but it was worth it. "We're doing what we should be doing now at the level of a world-class company," he says.

The key thing, Shaw adds, was the merging of IR and the business. "They were technology experts, and they had to become business experts," he says. "It's the only way to understand what you need to do and what the priorities are."

At Bowdoin College, Trust in IT Created a Culture of Change within a Haven of Liberal Arts

When Mitchel Davis made the decision in 2003 to move cross-country from California to Bowdoin College in Maine, it was to become one of the first CIO/senior officers for any liberal arts college in the United States. Even today, he explains, most colleges and universities don't position the CIO at the top of the organization.

It turned out to be a perfect storm for Davis and Bowdoin. He was looking for a place to test some of his ideas about how IT could drive change by providing exceptional services, consulting and leadership. And Bowdoin was looking to integrate technology into the liberal arts education. "I would have moved to China for this job," Davis says.

Davis's mission, according to Barry Mills, president of Bowdoin, was to make Bowdoin one of the most technically advanced liberal arts colleges in the country. He was charged with guiding the use of technology for teaching and research, leading the development of a comprehensive IT budget, overseeing the development of a Web strategy and evaluating the college's databases and systems and supervising their redesign and implementation, as needed.

When he arrived in Brunswick, Maine, however, Davis immediately saw a lot of things that needed to be changed before that could happen. There were six areas of IT, each of which competed for funding and had allegiances to different groups throughout the college, with no unification among them. In some cases, IT had ceded authority to certain computing resources, such as library servers and some that supported the academic deans. With this very siloed, politically-driven and non-collaborative structure, "You couldn't make an overall plan for how IT would run," Davis says.

Service, Davis says, "was the worst I'd ever seen." People had no clear idea of their job definition, and there was no standard level of service; instead, the level of service people received depended entirely on personal or political relationships. "I'd ask people how they were doing in their jobs, and they'd answer, 'I know I'm doing a good job, but I don't know how everyone else is doing,'" Davis says. "It was completely broken." The campus agreed, granting IT an approval rating of 10 percent in 2003.

"Our clients are intelligent people—they could see their IT support person was struggling, and they didn't see them as part of a team," concurs Rebecca Sandlin, deputy CIO at Bowdoin.

Overcoming Resistance

Davis was determined to keep as many of the current staff that he could and began the job of communicating the mission and vision of IT, as he saw it. He conducted a full staff and financial review, tore down the silos and began making plans for major projects such as a full network upgrade, a complete Web redesign and replacing old ERP software. It wasn't easy. "Very few people in IT bought in, and those who did, I promoted," he says. Others left. "The prospect of change was threatening," he says. "It was incredibly hostile. The president told me that people were in his office daily, saying I just wasn't being 'Bowdoin.'"

Still, Davis charged ahead, with the support of his senior leaders. He made it clear to the remaining staff that the changes he was making were supported from the highest levels of Bowdoin and that their jobs depended on making them. Davis says, "I had to have everyone concerned and let them know their job was at risk, to get them to stop thinking in terms of individual success and listen to what I was saying."

But for the transformation of IT to be successful, he knew that the entire staff, from the top down, needed to develop new skills and mindsets, in the areas of service, change management and marketing IT. He happened upon a book by Ouellette & Associates, called *IT at Your Service*, and he immediately bought enough copies to distribute to the entire staff.

"Someone finally put into words what I had thought all along about how IT needed to think about service," he says. "That whole concept of providing exceptional service to the client is the hardest thing to drive home."

Additionally, Davis and his leadership team completed O&A's workshops on building a service culture and became certified by O&A to teach these concepts to the internal staff over a three-year period of time. They started with the help desk, which adjusted quickly, Davis says; in fact, before he knew it, he received a call from one faculty member who previously was outwardly resistant to the changes being made in IT. This faculty member had called the help desk to ask for a USB thumb drive, expecting it to take six weeks. The service person asked when he needed it, and upon hearing that the faculty member's presentation was in a week, he offered him his own drive. "He called me and said, 'It's amazing—you've changed everything. These people are now trying to help us!'" Davis says.

238

This example, he says, shows that service is not about doing giant things but about the day-to-day interactions with clients and how you perceive your role in the organization. "Before, it was 'Go in, do it and get out,'" he says. "Now it's, 'I'm going to take the time to understand the client's needs so I can come up with a better idea of how to help them.'" The rest of Bowdoin has also noticed the change: IT's approval ratings shot up to 35 percent in 2004, from their low of 10 percent, and to 95 percent the following year.

The Fruits of Trust

Overall, Davis says, the IT staff has become well-tuned to client needs. Now, at the very beginning of any project, representatives from all parts of IT meet to discuss how the resulting changes will impact clients. "Everything is client-focused now," Sandlin says. "We couldn't do that before, when one group would change something on a system, and no one would even know about it."

The result: IT now enjoys new levels of credibility and trust. "Trust is something you receive for meeting or exceeding client expectations, while being empathetic and understanding to institutional, departmental and individual desires," Davis says.

With trust, IT has also gained more responsibility, a better sense of being valued and a new leadership role, Davis says. Case in point: IT is now always invited to departmental meetings, and it's included at the front end of all projects, whether in facilities, academics, or the business side of running the college, Davis says.

"If you have good working relationships with your partners in other departments and with your colleagues, then you can work with them in more of a consultative role," Sandlin says. "You understand what they're trying to do with their applications, and they're working side-by-side with you the whole time." This is a far cry from the old throw-it-over-the-wall mentality, she says, which resulted in lots of complaints and redos. Plus, clients start to gain an understanding of what IT does, "which leads to more appreciation for how the IT staff is spending their time," Sandlin says.

With the increased transparency, a number of staff and faculty oversight and advisory committees actually opted to disband, simply because IT was so transparent with budget, funding, projects, proposals, and results, Davis says. This has significantly decreased the amount of time it takes to make decisions, which results in big productivity increases.

IT also has its share of notoriety among students, who include articles about IT services and activities in the student paper on a weekly basis. When the topics get controversial, the level of trust that IT enjoys fully comes into play, Davis says. One recent article questioned IT's new practice of charging for their printing services. Collaborating with finance, IT was able to work with students to negotiate bulk rates and even promote the practice as a green initiative. "Students were bought-in so, they would drive it," he says.

The IT organization has also begun conducting business process reviews for various areas of the college, in order to deliver not just technology, but also performance improvements. This started in the financial department, when it requested a system upgrade, Davis says. "We wanted to understand what was being done before we brought new technology in there," he says. "Working closely with finance we noticed the college was interacting with seven different banks, and we got them down to three." Following that success, other business areas began inviting IT to look for similar process improvements.

Change-Positive Organizations

But the best outcome of developing a trusting relationship between IT and its campus clients was that it helped transform Bowdoin into a change-positive organization, Davis says. Davis first noticed this shift about four years after he began.

"Everything became easier to accomplish—clients were optimistically onboard and trusted IT to make decisions about business processes," he says. "Most people were actively anticipating the opportunity for IT to come in and do a business process assessment or work with faculty to actively support teaching and research," he says. This culture of change continues to spread across the college, he says. "IT is an engine of change, and almost everyone is onboard looking for opportunities."

Any conversation with a client is an opportunity to see how technology can help with their daily work life, Sandlin agrees. "We now have more time to do new and exciting things—we're out of reactive mode and can be progressive about looking for meaningful ways of using technology," she says. Case in point: A casual conversation with a professor recently led to in-class video chats with students studying abroad.

The desire for change, Davis says, has to begin with the CIO. "I've seen people go into a 'change' situation, but they haven't changed themselves, so they're still geared toward what the organization did three or four years ago," he says. Even in his own case, he says, Bowdoin no longer needs the CIO who arrived seven years ago—"now they need a high-level person who's thinking of ways to integrate technology across the organization and drive costs down," he says.

To support the momentum, Davis continues to hold refresher workshops each year, and he distributes copies of the book to new staff, other IT organizations, as well as vendors that work with Bowdoin. "My staff now leads these workshops, and they are actively attended," he says.

Change, like building trust, takes time, Davis says. "You can't expect things to happen overnight." In fact, much of what Bowdoin has been able to accomplish, he says, was created by the speed at which the culture could successfully absorb change, as well as massive communication and marketing efforts, team building and—at the very heart of all these efforts—exceptional client service.

Conclusion

These three stories are just a fraction of the IT culture changes and transformative journeys O&A has witnessed among our more than 3,000 clients. By adopting a consultative mindset and a client-focused, service orientation—as well as learning new skills in the areas of negotiating, project management, requirements gathering, political savvy, marketing, and leading change—our clients have become a model of the twenty-first century IT workforce.

We hope these inspiring success stories and the earlier chapters in the book have given you the tools and motivation to put the book into action so that your IT staff can similarly become a driving force behind your organization's success.

A Call to Action: Create Your Road Map for IT Transformation

At the beginning of this book, we recommended that you identify the two or three chapters that address the areas most pressing in your organization today. At the end of each chapter, we prompted you to capture the nuggets, action items, and so on that you found most timely and valuable.

Once you've completed the book, go back through the chapters and select the items you are going to act on. Demonstrate your commitment to your leadership team and staff by initiating activities and showing your willingness to see them through. Engage others in helping you develop strategies and action plans to address these priority items using the takeaways from that chapter. Don't forget to leverage the chapter you read on Change (Chapter 11), and your transformation journey will be well on its way.

Thank you for investing your time in reading *Unleashing the Power of IT: Bringing People, Business, and Technology Together* and our compliments to you for taking action to help take your organization, your team, and your career to the next level.

Good luck to you, and please don't hesitate to contact us if you have any questions along the way.

Bibliography

Ackerman-Anderson, Linda, and Dean Anderson. *Beyond Change Management*. San Francisco: Jossey-Bass, 2001.

Ackerman-Anderson, Linda, and Dean Anderson. *The Change Leader's Roadmap*. San Francisco: Jossey-Bass, 2001.

Acuff, Frank. *How to Negotiate Anything with Anyone Anywhere Around the World*. New York: AMACOM, 1997.

Albrecht, Karl, and Lawrence Bradford. *The Service Advantage*. New York: McGraw-Hill, 1989.

Albrecht, Karl, and Ron Yemke. *Service America!* New York: Grand Central Publishing, 1990.

Albrecht, Karl. *At America's Service*. New York: Grand Central Publishing, 1995.

Axelrod, Richard. *Terms of Engagement: Changing the Way We Change Organizations*. San Francisco: Berrett-Koehler, 2000.

Beck, Kent. *Extreme Programming Explained*. Boston: Addison-Wesley, 2000.

Berry, Leonard L. *Marketing Services*. New York: Free Press, 2004.

Block, Peter. *Flawless Consulting*. San Francisco: Pfeiffer, 1997.

Block, Thomas R., and J. Davidson Frame. *The Project Office*. Menlo Park, CA: Crisp Publications, 1998.

Bridges, William. *Managing Transitions: Making the Most of Change*. New York: Perseus Books, 1991.

Brinkman, Rick, and Rick Kirschner. *Dealing With People You Can't Stand*. New York: McGraw-Hill, 2002.

Broadbent, Marie, and Ellen S. Kitzis. *The New CIO Leader*. Boston: Harvard Business School Press, 2005.

Brooks, Dr. Michael. *The Power of Business Rapport*. New York: HarperCollins Publishers, 1991.

Brooks, Fred. *The Mythical Man-Month*. 2nd ed. Boston: Addison-Wesley, 1995.

Brown, Norm. "High-Leverage Best Practices," *Cutter IT Journal*. Cutter Corp., 1999.

Buckingham, Marcus. *Go Put Your Strengths to Work: 6 Powerful Steps to Achieve Outstanding Performance*. New York: Free Press, 2007.

Buckingham, Marcus. *First, Break All the Rules: What the World's Greatest Managers Do Differently*. New York: Simon & Schuster, 1999.

Buckingham, Marcus. *Now, Discover Your Strengths*. New York: Free Press, 2001.

Cantor, Murray R. *Object-Oriented Project Management with UML*. New York: John Wiley & Sons, 1998.

Carlzon, Jan. *Moments of Truth*. New York: Harper and Row, 1987.

Clarke, Boyd, and Ron Crossland. *The Leader's Voice*. New York: The Tom Peters Press and SelectBooks, 2002.

Cockburn, Alistair. *Surviving Object-Oriented Projects, A Manager's Guide*. Boston: Addison-Wesley, 1998.

Collins, Jim. *Good to Great: Why Some Companies Make the Leap . . . and Others Don't*. New York: HarperBusiness, 2001.

Conger, Jay A. "The Necessary Art of Persuasion," *Harvard Business Review*, May–June 1998.

Conner, Daryl R. *Managing at the Speed of Change*. New York: Random House, 1993.

Covey, Stephen R. *The 7 Habits of Highly Effective People*. New York: Free Press, 2004.

DeLuca, Joel R. *Political Savvy; Systematic Approaches to Leadership Behind the Scenes.* Berwyn, PA: The Evergreen Business Group, 1999.

Demarco, Tom, and Timothy Lister. *Peopleware—Productive Projects and Teams.* New York: Dorset House, 1999.

DeMarco, Tom. *Controlling Software Projects.* New York: Yourdon Press, 1982.

DeMarco, Tom. *The Deadline.* New York: Dorset House, 1997.

Denning, Stephen. *The Leader's Guide to Storytelling: Mastering the Art and Discipline of Business Narrative.* San Francisco: Jossey-Bass, 2005.

Dobson, Michael, and Deborah Dobson. *Enlightened Office Politics.* New York: AMACOM, 2001.

Duck, Jeanie Daniel. *The Change Monster.* New York: Crown Business, 2001.

Eccles, Robert, and Nitin Nohria. *Beyond the Hype: Rediscovering the Essence of Management.* Boston: The Harvard Business School Press, 1992.

Emerick, Donald, and K. Round. *Exploring Web Marketing and Project Management.* Upper Saddle River, NJ: Prentice-Hall, 1999.

Fairhurst, Gail T., and Robert A. Sarr. *The Art of Framing: Managing the Language of Leadership.* San Francisco: Jossey-Bass, 1996.

Farson, Richard. *Management of the Absurd.* New York: Simon and Schuster, 1997.

Ferrazzi, Keith, and Tahl Raz. *Never Eat Alone: And Other Secrets to Success, One Relationship at a Time.* New York: Doubleday Business, 2005.

Fisher, Roger, and Allen Sharp. *Getting It Done.* New York: HarperCollins, 1998.

Fisher, Roger, and William Ury. *Getting to Yes: Negotiating Agreements without Giving In.* New York: Penguin, 1991.

Frame, J. Davidson. *Project Management Competence*. San Francisco: Jossey-Bass, 1999.

Friedman, Thomas L. *The World Is Flat: A Brief History of the Twenty-First Century*. New York: Farrar, Straus and Giroux, 2005.

Gardiner, Gareth. *Tough-Minded Management*. New York: Ballantine Books, 1990.

Gardner, Howard. *Changing Minds: The Art and Science of Changing Our Own and Other People's Minds*. Boston: Harvard Business School Press, 2004.

Gladwell, Malcolm. *The Tipping Point: How Little Things Can Make a Big Difference*. New York: Little, Brown and Company, 2000.

Goldratt, Dr. Eliyahu M. *Critical Chain*. Great Barrington, MA: North River Press, 1997.

Goldratt, Dr. Eliyahu M. *The Goal*. 2nd ed. Great Barrington, MA: North River Press, 1992.

Goleman, Daniel. *Working with Emotional Intelligence*. New York: Bantam Books, 2000.

Grady, Robert. *Practical Software Metrics for PM and Process Improvement*. Upper Saddle River, NJ: Prentice-Hall, 1992.

Graham, Robert, and R. Englund. *Creating an Environment for Successful Projects*. San Francisco: Jossey-Bass, 1997.

Greene, Robert. *The 48 Laws of Power*. New York: Penguin, 2000.

Greiner, Larry, and Virginia Schein. *Power and Organizational Development: Mobilizing Power to Implement Change*. Boston: Addison-Wesley, 1988.

Harvard Business Essentials. *Power, Influence, and Persuasion*. Boston: Harvard Business School Press, 2005.

Haynes, Marion E. *Effective Meeting Skills*. Mississauga, ON, Canada: Crisp Learning, 1997.

Holden, Mark. *Positive Politics*. Warriewood, NSW, Australia: Business and Professional Publishing, 1998.

Jacobs, Paula, "Negotiating for Success." *Infoworld,* December 7, 1998.

Jacobson, I., G. Booch, and J. Rumbaugh. *Unified Software Development Process.* Boston: Addison-Wesley, 1999.

Johnson, Spencer. *Who Moved My Cheese.* London, UK: Vermilion, 2002.

Jones, Capers. *Patterns of Software Systems Failure and Success.* London, UK: Thomson Computer Press, 1995.

Jones, Capers. *Software Assessments, Benchmarks, and Best Practices.* Boston: Addison-Wesley, 2000.

Katzenbach, Jon R., and Douglas K. Smith. *The Wisdom of Teams.* New York: HarperBusiness, 1994.

Kerzner, Harold. *Project Management: A Systems Approach.* New York: John Wiley & Sons, 1998.

Knight, Christopher. *Top 7 Ways to Get the Most From Negotiating Via Email. Top7Business.com,* 2003.

Kotter, John P. *Leading Change.* Boston: Harvard Business School Press, 1996.

Kübler-Ross, Elizabeth. *On Death and Dying.* New York: Macmillan, 1969.

Lancaster, Hal, "You Have to Negotiate for Everything in Life, So Get Good at It." *Wall Street Journal,* January 27, 1998.

Lencioni, Patrick. *The Five Dysfunctions of a Team.* San Francisco: Jossey-Bass, 2002.

Lencioni, Patrick. *Silos, Politics and Turf Wars.* San Francisco: Jossey-Bass, 2006.

Lencioni, Patrick. *Death by Meeting.* San Francisco: Jossey-Bass, 2004.

Lewis, James P. *Mastering Project Management.* New York: McGraw-Hill, 1998.

Lill, David, and Robin Peterson. "Negotiation Tactics." *Personal Selling Power,* January/February, 1993.

Lundin, Stephen C. *Fish! A Remarkable Way to Boost Morale and Improve Results.* New York: Hyperion, 2000.

Lundin, Stephen, John Christensen, and Harry Paul. *Fish! Sticks*. New York: Hyperion, 2003.

Maitra, Amit K. *Internet Solutions for Project Managers*. New York: John Wiley & Sons, 2000.

McCarthy, Jim. *Dynamics of Software Development*. Redmond, WA: Microsoft Press, 1995.

McConnell, Steve. *Rapid Development*. Redmond, WA: Microsoft Press, 1996.

McIntyre, Marie G. *Secrets to Winning at Office Politics: How to Achieve Your Goals and Increase Your Influence at Work*. New York: St. Martin's Griffin, 2005.

Merlyn, Vaughan, and John Parkinson. *Development Effectiveness*. New York: John Wiley & Sons, 1994.

Mnookin, Robert. *Negotiation: The Advanced Course*. New York: Across the Board, 2002.

Morrison, Terri, Wayne Conaway, and George Borden. *Kiss, Bow, or Shake Hands*. Avon, MA: Adams Media Corporation, 1994.

Nevis, Edwin C. et al. *Intentional Revolutions: A Seven-Point Strategy for Transforming Organizations*. San Francisco: Jossey-Bass, 1996.

Newbold, Robert C. *Project Management in the Fast Lane*. New York: St. Lucie Press, 1998.

Nicholson, Nigel. "How Hardwired Is Human Behavior?" *Harvard Business Review*, July–August 1998.

Oakley, Ed, and Doug Krug. *Enlightened Leadership*. New York: Simon and Schuster, 1991.

Ouellette, L. Paul. *IT at Your Service*. Dubuque, IA: Kendall-Hunt Publishing, 1993.

Parker, Glenn M. *Cross-Functional Teams*. San Francisco: Jossey-Bass, 1994.

Patterson, Kerry, Joseph Grenny, Ron McMillan, and Al Switzler. *Crucial Conversations: Tools for Talking When Stakes Are High*. New York: McGraw-Hill, 2002.

Patterson, Kerry, Joseph Grenny, David Maxfield, Ron McMillan, and Al Switzler. *Influencer: The Power to Change Anything.* New York: McGraw-Hill, 2008.

Patching, Keith, and Robina Chatham. *Corporate Politics for IT Managers.* Burlington, MA: Butterworth-Heinemann, 2000.

Pinto, Jeffrey K. *Power and Politics in Project Management.* Boston: Project Management Institute, 1996.

Project Management Institute. *A Guide to the Project Management Body of Knowledge.* Boston: Project Management Institute, 2004.

Quinn, Robert E., *Deep Change.* San Francisco: Jossey-Bass, 1996.

Rackman, Neil. *The Behavior of Successful Negotiators.* Yorkshire, UK: Huthwaite Research Ltd., 1980.

Reardon, Kathleen Kelley. *The Secret Handshake.* New York: Doubleday, 2000.

Robbins, Harvey. *Why Teams Don't Work.* Princeton, NJ: Peterson's/Pacesetter Books, 1995.

Royce, Walker. *Software Project Management, A Unified Framework.* Boston: Addison-Wesley, 1998.

Sample, Steven B. *The Contrarian's Guide to Leadership.* San Francisco: Jossey-Bass, 2002.

Scheier, Robert. "20 Ways to Avoid Getting Hyped into a Bad Deal." *Computerworld,* September 23, 1996.

Schneider, Polly. "Finding the Right Chemistry." *CIO,* November 1, 1998.

Senge, Peter. *The Dance of Change.* New York: Doubleday, 1999.

Shell, Richard G. *Bargaining for Advantage: Negotiation Strategies for Reasonable People.* New York: Penguin Group, 2006.

Simmons, Annette. *The Story Factor: Secrets of Influencing from the Art of Storytelling.* New York: Basic Books, 2001.

Steinberg, Robert. *Chess v. Poker: What Is Your Style of Negotiation?* Mediate.com, June 2003.

Thomas, Kenneth, and Ralph Kilmann. *Thomas-Kilmann Conflict Mode Instrument.* Tuxedo Park, NY: Xicom, 1974.

Ury, William. *Getting Past No: Negotiating in Difficult Situations.* New York: Bantam Books, 1993.

Von Oech, Roger. *A Whack on the Side of the Head.* New York: Business Plus, 1998.

Weinberg, Gerald. *Quality Software Management.* Vol. 2. New York: Dorset House, 1993.

Whitaker, Ken. *Managing Software Maniacs.* New York: John Wiley & Sons, Inc., 1994.

About the Contributors

Carolynn Benson (Chapter 9) is a senior facilitator and consultant with O&A with extensive experience in the areas of internal consulting, client service, negotiating, presentation skills, corporate politics, and marketing. One of her key strengths is helping clients build a more consultative, client-focused culture. Before joining O&A, Carolynn worked for 17 years in high tech in a number of management, consulting, and sales and marketing capacities.

Charlie Duczakowski (Chapter 7) is a senior O&A facilitator and consultant who specializes in business requirements gathering and management, modeling, metrics, project management, and business process reengineering. He brings a unique blend of knowledge in the fields of system analysis and functional metrics, with a wealth of practical, hands-on experience in both writing and managing requirements. Before joining O&A, Charlie was a consultant for Capers Jones's Software Productivity Research. He also served as a director, business analyst and project manager, director of systems development, and director of relationship management and systems analysis at Fidelity Investments.

Kenneth Emery (Chapter 10) is a senior facilitator and consultant with O&A. He has been recognized as a highly skilled senior executive with strong strategic planning and change management experience in diverse industries. He has effectively leveraged IT to enable organizational growth, change, and profitability. Before joining O&A, Ken was senior vice president of information management and shared services for CPS Energy, the largest municipally owned utility in the United States.

Greg Fouquet, PMP, CCP, CISA (Chapter 6) is a senior O&A facilitator and consultant who has spent the past 15 years helping organizations in numerous industries improve the productivity, satisfaction, and overall success of their business and IT projects. Before O&A, Greg spent four years at Ernst & Young's national office as a senior manager and project director in the company's advanced technology group. He also has more than 15 years of IT management experience as vice president and manager of a 160-person IT department, senior group project manager, senior systems analyst, and lead EDP auditor.

Laura Gorman (Chapter 4) is a senior facilitator and consultant for O&A with extensive experience in the areas of leading change, internal consulting, client service, meeting management, and leadership. Her strengths are in facilitating the development and implementation of change management strategies. Before joining O&A, Laura was a senior consultant with a large Midwestern insurance and financial services company, for which she was a consultant to the IT department.

Bill Hagerup (Chapter 8), has been in IT for more than 30 years. He has held numerous leadership roles and worked in the trenches of systems development, client support, and computer operations. He's adept at leading both software development and organizational transformation projects and demonstrates natural talents as an instructor and facilitator. Before joining O&A, Bill worked for a consulting company for which he led numerous IT culture change efforts, and at a large insurance company, as vice president of organizational effectiveness.

Anita Leto (Chapter 3) has been a senior facilitator and consultant for O&A for the past 16 years. She has extensive experience in internal client service, IT marketing, consulting, team building, and leadership. She facilitates sessions for senior IT leaders in the areas of strategic and tactical planning, GAP analysis, and culture change. Anita is known for her keen ability to understand a company's existing culture and provide specific action plans on how to evolve to their desired culture. Before O&A, Anita worked for Canon, Inc. and Unisys Corp., where she held a variety of managerial positions.

Dan Roberts (Chapter 1) joined O&A in 1986 and has been its president since 1995. He strategizes with IT and business executives and their leadership teams across North America on issues relating to transitioning their IT cultures from reactive, technology-centric order takers to consultative, client-focused providers of choice.

Gwen Walsh (Chapter 2) is a senior consultant with more than 25 years of experience in leadership development and organization reinvention. She helps clients create and sustain execution-based cultures focused on delivering results and attaining performance targets, shaping and instilling leadership competencies and behaviors, increasing profitability and competitive advantage, optimizing human capital investments, and driving down expenses. Before O&A, Gwen served as CIO and partner for Christian & Timbers, a large executive search firm, and as director of IS at Medical Mutual.

Lisha Wentworth (Chapter 5) has been a senior facilitator and consultant at O&A since the late 1980s. She is an experienced IT instructor, course developer, and consultant in the areas of IT client service, internal consulting, negotiating and communicating, and marketing. Lisha is known for her energy, humor, and ability to connect with and engage an audience. Before joining O&A, she served as a project manager at a nationally known health insurance provider and at a large New England–based insurance company.

About O&A

Ouellette & Associates Consulting, Inc. has worked with more than 3,000 IT and shared-service organizations since our founding in 1984. *Unleashing the Power of IT: Bringing People, Business, and Technology Together* has been years in the making and is based on this extensive real-world experience. The following are a few of the resources and services that our clients leverage in support of their transformation, culture change, and professional development initiatives:

IT Leadership Services

- Organization Assessment
- Leadership Assessment and Coaching
- Strategy Development and Execution
- Project Advisory Services

IT Leadership Development

- Leading Change across IT and the Enterprise
- Managing Vendor Partnerships
- Marketing the IT Organization Internally
- Strategic Sourcing

IT Professional Development Series

- Achieving IT Service Excellence
- Consulting Skills for the IT Professional
- Partnering for Success: Leadership and Communication Skills

- Internal Negotiating Skills for the IT Professional
- Presentation Skills for the IT Professional

IT Project Management and Business Analyst Development

- Project Management Certificate Program
- Business Analyst Certificate Program
- IT Project Management: The Human Side of the Equation
- Advanced Project Management
- The Politics of IT Project Management
- Business Requirements Management
- Testing for Business Analysts

If you would like to learn more about these customized, IT-specific services and how you can leverage them as your road map for building your twenty-first century workforce and culture, please contact us at 800-878-4551 or info@ouellette-online.com.

Index